Energy Futures of Developing Countries

An Aspen Institute Book

Energy Futures of Developing Countries

The Neglected Victims of the Energy Crisis

EDITED BY HARLAN CLEVELAND

PRAEGER SPECIAL STUDIES • PRAEGER SCIENTIFIC

Published in 1980 by Praeger Publishers
CBS Educational and Professional Publishing
A Division of CBS, Inc.
521 Fifth Avenue, New York, New York 10017 U.S.A.

0123456789   056   987654321

Library of Congress Cataloging in Publication Data

Aspen Institute Workshop on Energy Futures of
    Developing Countries, Cairo, 1979.
    Energy futures of developing countries.

    At head of title: Aspen Institute for Humanistic
Studies, Program in International Affairs.
    1. Underdeveloped areas—Energy policy—Congresses.
I. Cleveland, Harlan. II. Aspen Institute Program
on International Affairs. III. Title.
HD9502.A2A76   1979   333.79'09172'4   80-10702
ISBN 0-03-058669-0

Printed in the United States of America

Contents

List of Abbreviations

BTU	British thermal unit
CGIAR	Consultative Group on International Agricultural Research
CIEC	Conference on International Economic Cooperation
DOE	Department of Energy
FAO	Food and Agriculture Organization
GNP	Gross National Product
IAEA	International Atomic Energy Agency
IDA	International Development Association
IEA	International Energy Agency
IFAD	International Fund for Agricultural Development
IFED	International Fund for Energy Development
IMF	International Monetary Fund
INFCE	International Nuclear Fuel Cycle Evaluation
INTELSAT	International Telecommunications Satellite
KW	Kilowatt
KWe	Kilowatt of electricity
KWh	Kilowatt hour
LDC	Less developed countries
LNG	Liquid natural gas
MBD	Millions of barrels per day
MBDOE	Million barrels per day oil equivalent
MW	Megawatt
NIC	Newly Industrialized Country
OAPEC	Organization of Arab Petroleum Exporting Countries
ODC	Overseas Development Council
ODCOI	Organization of Developing Countries— Oil Importing
OECD	Organization for Economic Cooperation and Development
OIDC	Oil importing developing country
OLADE	Latin American Energy Organization
OPEC	Organization of Petroleum Exporting Countries
PRC	People's Republic of China
PVC	Photo voltaic cell
Quad	Quadrillion BTUs
SDR	Special drawing rights
SEDF	Solar Energy Development Fund
SRE	Small scale renewable energy
UNDP	United Nations Development Program
USAID	United States Agency for International Development
Wpk	Peak watt

Foreword

An Aspen Institute workshop on Energy Futures of Developing Countries was held in Cairo, Egypt, from January 26 to 30, 1979. It was initiated by the Aspen Institute's Committee on Energy Policy; cosponsored by the Institute's Middle East project, the al Dir'iyyah Institute of Geneva (Switzerland) and the Institute of National Planning in Cairo; managed by the Aspen Institute's Program in International Affairs; and cochaired by Ibrahim H. Abdel Rahman and myself. A list of those participating in the workshop will be found in the Appendix.

The workshop opened with substantive addresses by the Egyptian Ministers of Planning and of Electricity and Power, and by the Undersecretary of the Ministry of Petroleum. Local arrangements were courteously and efficiently handled by the Institute of National Planning.

For the occasion, a comprehensive discussion paper, "South-North Cooperation on Energy for Development," was commissioned by the Aspen Institute to the Overseas Development Council, and prepared by James W. Howe, James J. Tarrant III and Julie A. Martin. An updated version of this paper constitutes a major element of this report.

Also made available to the workshop participants were several current publications on the energy scene, including the Trilateral Commission's *Energy: Managing the Transition* by John Sawhill, Keichi Oshima and Hanns Maull; the Rockefeller Foundation's *International Energy Supply: A Perspective from the Industrial World* by Melvin Conant; Walter Levy's "The Years that the Locust Hath Eaten: Development" (*Foreign Affairs*, Winter 1978-9), and *A Note on Research: Energy for Developing Countries* by Lincoln Gordon of Resources for the Future.

Kirit S. Parikh of India and James W. Howe of the United States served as joint rapporteurs for the Cairo workshop. Their joint report is part of the present publication. Some comments by the cochairman, also written after the Cairo workshop, will be found in an introductory essay.

After the workshop, I developed a proposal for international arrangements designed to make sure that oil-importing developing countries could get access to their minimum essential requirements of oil at times of acute shortage. This paper was transmitted to U.S. government officials by Joseph E. Slater, President of the Aspen Institute, on behalf of a group that included John Sawhill, Thornton F. Bradshaw, Eric Zausner, Paul Doty, Waldemar Nielsen and myself. The text of that proposal is also included in this report.

Harlan Cleveland

Aspen Institute for Humanistic Studies
Program in International Affairs

CHAPTER ONE   INTRODUCTION

The Neglected Victims
of the Energy Crisis

I.H. ABDEL RAHMAN

AND HARLAN CLEVELAND

I

Everyone seems to agree that "energy futures of developing countries" is
the neglected corner of world energy planning. The oil importing developing countries have been hit hard by rising prices of the oil and other
imports they need for development. The impressive political solidarity of
the Third World caucus (the "Group of 77") in international organizations
tends to obscure the highly varied problems faced by individual countries
as they take the measure of their "energy futures."

Inside most developing countries there are two very different energy
economies: the modern sector that figures in the world energy balance
(which usually counts only energy for commercial use and in international
trade) and the rural sector based mostly on wood fuel, crop residues,
dung, animal draft power and human effort directly applied. Oil, gas, coal
and electricity account for only one-third of India's energy; in some countries, the ratio of non-commercial to commercial fuels may be as high as
nine to one. Remarkably little hard information exists on the demand for
and supply of traditional forms of energy.

Oil and gas will evidently be "available" through the end of the century
and probably beyond; that is, the world is not going to "run out" of oil and
gas. But it will be more and more costly. Those developing nations that
have oil, gas or coal in their ground had better place a very high priority on
finding and developing it. Coal imports are not likely to be a big part of the
energy futures of developing countries; neither is nuclear energy, except
in a few large industrial areas. Hydro power, still largely lacking in most
developing countries, has a brighter future than generally has been cre-
dited in recent world energy analyses.

"Solar energy," including not only wind and direct use of sunlight but
especially biological forms of energy, will obviously not play a big role for

1

the time being. But it is worth much more attention in research and development to make sure its advantages (which include more equitable distribution around the world than conventional fuels) are realized in a major way by the end of the century and beyond. Decentralized and exotic energy tend to be given short shrift in R & D priorities in industrial countries preoccupied with centralized power production and its distribution as electricity through interconnected grids.

II

Events since the Cairo meeting was held, most importantly the Iranian revolution and the 1979 rounds of OPEC price increases, have restored energy to the top priority status that most governments had briefly accorded it in 1973 and 1974. Lulled into complacency by a period of stable prices and more than adequate supplies of oil during the intervening years, both the industrialized nations of the "North" and the developing nations of the "South," particularly those which import oil, were rudely reintroduced in 1979 to an era of uncertain oil supplies available only at sharply increased prices.

The industrialized nations, the largest consumers of oil, are beginning to readjust their economic and political policies to include energy in a more comprehensive and rational manner. The results of the Tokyo summit (June 1979) and the subsequent actions of the United States, as well as declarations of increased reliance on alternatives to oil by nations such as Brazil, suggest that the governments of nations with large industrial sectors have realized the necessity to adopt more farseeing energy policies.

For the oil importing developing nations the problem is more acute. Generally lacking the resources and technology needed to adjust their development policies away from dependence on oil, these nations are the most severely affected by the rising prices and uncertainty of supply. Because many of them are also net food importers, their situation is further compounded, especially since they have no real say in future pricing and supply decisions made by the world's major food exporters—the U.S., Canada and Australia. Often chronically short of capital and foreign exchange needed to purchase both oil and food, these countries face the dire choice of having to decide between the two—with terrible sacrifices almost a certainty in either case.

Perhaps the most direct effect of the precarious position of oil importing developing nations will be a political threat to the solidarity of the South. While the stalling of the North-South dialogue and the disappointing results of the UNCTAD meeting in Manila (May-June 1979) did not raise a serious challenge to that solidarity, the plight of the oil importing nations is more immediately pressing. If the nations of the developing world are to be more fully incorporated into the global economic and political systems, the continuing unity of the South appears to remain a necessity for those countries and for the world as a whole.

The clear implication of all this is a need for international cooperation. Long term national and international measures are needed to adjust to the new energy uncertainties. Conservation will be a top priority for all countries. Those nations that can afford it must explore alternative sources of energy. All nations, North and South, must adopt comprehensive energy policies which relate more directly to their development and growth policies. The most urgent task of all is to achieve some form of agreement and cooperation to assure the continuous flow of vital world commodities. Without such international action, the problems we see in the present will almost certainly be intensified in the future.

The problem of the oil importing developing nations, although extremely important, is just one example of the need for international support for the "hard cases" of development—the poorest countries and, within countries, the neediest segments of their populations. Unless effective national and international measures are taken now, the circumstances of this decade—rapidly increasing prices for energy, food and other essential commodities—will simply grow worse. Whether the UN Third Decade of Development, the 1980s, is to be one of progress or regression will in large part depend on international measures taken now to alleviate the impact, especially on the least developed nations, of global economic disruptions. It will be essential to ensure for such countries the resources (including aid) to avoid the more serious calamities which could upset the critical balance of world peace and security.

III

From four days of talk about these issues in Cairo last January emerged something like a consensus to give a much higher priority to—but no consensus on how to organize—the following functions:

• Contingency planning for periods of acute scarcity, and a system designed to assure fair access to scarce resources by all countries, including the oil importing developing countries (OIDCs).

• The funding of indigenous energy exploration and development, to which trans-national enterprise can make a major contribution within "rules of the game" that need to be defined.

• Arrangements to make sure that the world's research and development talent is directed toward the OIDCs' energy problems and strategies.

• A focus on, and incentives to promote, energy conservation by

OIDCs—without pushing conservation so hard as to be a drag on development.

• Special studies (with a view to action) of rural energy supply, including the development of energy from biomass and techniques for avoiding further deforestation.

• Efforts to generate regional arrangements for mutual self-reliance.

• An international analytical ("policy planning") capacity to (a) develop authoritative and comparative statistics on energy and development; (b) consider the connection between energy strategies and equity ("basic needs") strategies in developing countries, and (c) conduct policy analysis of OIDC energy alternatives, including both the technological options and the issues of "sociological acceptance" to which they give rise.

Not adequately discussed at our Cairo meeting, but most important in the short run, is the financing of oil imports as such. The existing pile-up of OIDC debt, and the prospect that oil, though available, will keep becoming more expensive, requires urgent international attention to the financing of imported energy for development.

There was no meeting of the minds on how all these functions should be organized at the international level. Some support was voiced for tackling each of them *ad hoc* through existing public and non-governmental agencies; for converting the International Atomic Energy Agency (IAEA) into a world energy agency; or for establishing a world energy agency from scratch (folding in, or leaving outside as essentially a security function, the nuclear safeguards function of IAEA).

On one point, however, there did seem to be agreement which was both broad and deep: Governmental negotiation about these issues, in a revived "North-South dialogue" or otherwise, is not going to get anywhere unless and until the interested non-governmental communities lay the groundwork for official action through unofficial consultations such as our Cairo meeting and the professional and analytical work that should now follow from it.

The Need for Action

KARIT S. PARIKH AND JAMES W. HOWE

PART I: THE WORLD ENERGY SCENE

1. GLOBAL PARAMETERS

There is substantial consensus among oil experts that oil and gas supply will be increasing through the end of this century, after which it will decline. However, during this time, demand will also be increasing and will drive up real prices. When supply starts to decrease, it will not give out suddenly but will decline slowly, leading to further price rises.

Reserves of coal are plentiful, but because international trade in coal is not very practical with the present infrastructure, it is unlikely to take the place of oil. Moreover, the potential of coal is not yet known for many developing countries; and there are, of course, environmental drawbacks to coal as well.

Nuclear power plants are usually built in units too large to be suitable for most developing countries, with the possible exception of a few of their large urban industrial complexes. Nuclear power plants can be built in smaller units as is done in India. Nevertheless, nuclear energy is unlikely to be a major source of energy for the developing countries in the foreseeable future. Renewable energy forms, photovoltaics, solar collectors, windmills, bio digesters and other more exotic options give reason for hope; but they are still largely untested and most of them are still costly compared with oil based technologies. Thus, such options are unlikely to play a major role in meeting the energy needs in the immediate future. Though there is some room to expand the supply of some of the traditional sources (e.g. wood, crop and animal wastes, and animal traction) through careful management and improved technology, this would require capital and organizational skills, both of which are scarce in developing countries.

2. ENERGY SCENE IN THE DEVELOPING COUNTRIES

The developing countries are not a homogeneous lot. They include oil exporting countries, oil importing countries and oil self-sufficient countries. A few have indigenous coal production but most countries' coal reserves are not even known. Many countries depend substantially on the traditional non-commercial forms of fuel for their energy requirements,

5

but there are also some countries which largely use commercial energy. The commercial energy based on oil, coal and electricity is used predominantly by modern industries and residences centered in major cities. The traditional (largely renewable) sources, in countries where these are important, are used by the majority who inhabit farms, villages, smaller towns, urban slums and the non-commercial sectors of urban areas.

Developing countries as a group consume very little commercial energy (only about 18 percent of the global total). Nevertheless, many developing countries rely largely on oil for their commercial energy needs. The price of imported oil as well as the prices of a number of non-oil imports to developing countries have gone up; in many cases, the latter have risen faster than the price of oil, and this has posed severe problems to developing countries in financing their imports of oil and other items vital for development.

Another serious aspect of the energy crisis in the developing world is the shortage of fuel to burn in the non-commercial rural and urban sector. Forests are being depleted as the search for fuel results in much unplanned felling of trees. Animal dung is burned rather than used as manure and is thus not returned to the soil. These practices have led to soil erosion, fertility reduction and desertification.

PART II: ENERGY PROBLEMS OF LESS DEVELOPED COUNTRIES AND INDICATED ACTIONS

1. ENERGY DEMAND AND NEEDS

Very little is known about the use of traditional energy in most developing countries, or about the trends in the supply of traditional energy. Information is inadequate even regarding commercial energy in the developing world. The only way to fill data gaps is to collect data, yet some policy decisions cannot wait till that is done. New methods of projecting energy demand and needs are required. These methods should embody the policy instruments in them, so that policies required to realize the demand and supply projection of a particular scenario are made explicit.

Suggested Actions:

a) The relevant energy demand studies carried out for various developing countries should be pooled, and a "do it yourself" manual should be prepared in loose leaf form (so that it can be updated as understanding improves) outlining how to carry out demand studies for developing countries and how to gather data especially in rural areas;

b) At the same time studies to refine survey and projection methods should be promoted;

c) Studies on a regional basis should be promoted to identify areas of regional cooperation. In these studies there is a need to emphasize rural energy.

2. FINANCING OIL AND OTHER IMPORTS WITH RISING COSTS

Energy is so important to development that energy importing developing countries (most of them import oil) must give energy imports a high priority even when energy prices rise. Oil prices are expected to increase in the future. It is unlikely that oil will be sold at a price to developing countries different from the price at which it is sold to developed countries. No major traded good is traded that way. Some subsidy is available for oil imports through the IMF in the form of credit at better than market terms. Beyond that, and beyond some credit extended bilaterally by individual oil exporting countries, the oil importing developing countries will have to earn the money to pay for oil and other imports through increased exports.

Actions:
a) The rest of the countries in the world and particularly the developed countries must open their markets to the exports of the oil importing developing countries and ensure a fair price;
b) Additional IMF and other international credits should be made available to finance critical energy imports of the developing countries.

3. SECURITY OF OIL SUPPLY TO OIL IMPORTING DEVELOPING COUNTRIES

The Third World needs oil for high priority development purposes. There is little scope for reduction in demand because there is little luxury use of oil. If supply from one or more of the major producers were interrupted for a few months, oil importing developing countries would face a crisis in their economic life. OECD countries have a plan for such a contingency whereby oil would be allocated with some degree of equity among the members of OECD. Because the global oil allocating mechanisms are controlled by the developed countries, there is some concern that the oil importing developing countries would not get a fair share in a case of a supply interruption. Moreover, if oil prices were to rise substantially over a short period in a crisis, some of the developing countries may be put to great hardship. Of course, oil is not the only commodity whose supply might be interrupted. The difference is that oil is more crucial to economic health and development than other goods.

Action:
A mechanism is required for allocating oil in a crisis to the developing

countries with a higher priority than to developed countries. An appropriate mechanism should be devised and promoted for this purpose.

4. ENERGY SUPPLY FOR RURAL AND FOR URBAN "TRADITIONAL" AREAS

People in the rural and urban "traditional" areas use wood or charcoal and animal and crop wastes for cooking and heating, as do backyard industries for process heat. One result is increasing deforestation, a continuing decline in soil fertility along with soil erosion and downstream flooding. Reforestation schemes have faced many problems, including the need (particularly in badly deforested areas) to protect new trees from people desperate for fuel to cook their food. Clearly, a part of such protection is to make available an alternate fuel during the growth period of the newly planted trees. However, such alternate fuel systems must be within the economic reach of poor people. Many alternative technical solutions suggested for rural decentralized energy systems have not been successful because of inadequate attention to economic and institutional factors.

Actions:

a) The experiences of different countries with past failures and successes of technologies that may serve as alternatives to unplanned use of wood should be compiled. Such technologies include bio gas and solar wood plantations. Manuals should be prepared which would give guidelines for evaluating the feasibility of such alternative technologies, not only as to their technical and economic practicality but also from the point of view of institutional acceptability;

b) Research and development for alternative technologies should be promoted;

c) New technologies in the R & D laboratories should be tested through pilot projects for reactions of the users about its convenience of use and appropriateness in the social and economic contexts. Pilot projects and site tests should be promoted;

d) Concerted international action to promote rapid diffusion of alternatives that have been tested successfully through pilot projects is required. Such actions may involve subsidizing conventional fuels that may be needed pending development of the new alternatives designed to provide long term solutions;

e) Areas should be identified in which reforestation can be carried out without the danger of the new plants being uprooted by people in search of firewood. In these areas, reforestation drives should be promoted.

5. CONSERVATION OF ENERGY IN THE DEVELOPING COUNTRIES

Even though the very rich in the developing countries do waste energy in luxury consumption, the rich are few in number, and their conservation will contribute only marginally. Any effort at conservation beyond this, which reduces effective consumption, is likely to lead to a slowdown in development for many developing countries. The major scope for conservation in the developing countries is reducing the inefficient use of energy. For example, present cooking in rural and urban-traditional areas is often done over open fires which may be no more than 5 percent efficient. More efficient cooking stoves could double or triple efficiency. Yet introducing improved stoves would not be an easy task.

Actions:

a) More R & D is needed on development of efficient stoves, which are made of local materials cheap enough for poor people to buy and which are convenient enough in the context of their environment so that they will want to buy them;

b) The more promising stoves should be site-tested for local acceptibility and performance;

c) International and national action should be mobilized to diffuse rapidly such acceptable models in critical areas of developing countries.

6. RESEARCH AND DEVELOPMENT

The energy R & D of the world is concentrated almost entirely in the developed countries. Most of this research is directed to the needs of the developed countries. Apart from the fact that most of this research is not appropriate for meeting the energy needs of the developing countries, this concentration of research in the developed countries poses the danger that the high technology required for the post-oil transition period will become a monopoly of the developed countries. Although growing rapidly, R & D in all forms of renewable energy is still meager, with about 70 percent of it in the United States. Only a small but unknown fraction is devoted to small-scale renewable energy systems of the kind that might be appropriate for the needs of developing countries. R & D—particularly adaptive R & D—in the universities and research institutes of the developing countries is growing. But there are no global or regional mechanisms for coordinating this work to avoid duplication and to maximize effectiveness.

Actions:

a) There should be an increase in joint R & D projects with teams involving researchers and institutions from both the developed and the developing countries. In such projects, the definition and identification of R & D tasks should also be carried out jointly and as much work should be carried out in the developing countries as possible;

b) More cooperative R & D among developing countries needs to be promoted;

c) An institutional mechanism needs to be developed for sharing knowledge throughout the world and for facilitating a new flow of energy research-generated information from North to South and (in certain cases such as methane generation and alcohol production) from South to North.

7. DEVELOPMENT OF INDIGENOUS ENERGY RESOURCES

Large areas of many developing countries are as yet unexplored for energy resources, and a great deal of oil, gas and coal may yet remain to be found and developed. Similarly, there is a great deal of renewable energy in the form of sunlight, wind, water resources and organic mass. Development of these resources is hindered by a lack of technological and managerial skills to explore and exploit this energy. Countries with weak infrastructure, small markets and modest geological prospects have difficulty persuading private oil companies to give them high priority on reasonable terms. A measure of self-reliance is thus called for, yet the problem of finding adequate finance remains. Some of the international funding agencies have recently recognized this problem and are making limited amounts of capital available for development; a small amount is available for exploration.

In the case of major hydroelectric projects, in addition to a lack of finance and technological skills, problems of inter-regional or international cooperation among two or more countries have retarded development. Even when a hydro development benefits all countries concerned, the difficulties of working out agreements on sharing the benefits have prevented starting of a number of very promising hydro projects.

Actions:

a) More finance should be provided for energy projects including energy exploration. Technical assistance should be geared to creating self-reliance in the recipient country;

b) Cooperation in the development of international rivers should be promoted. In this context, studies that quantify and explain the "positive-sum game" benefits of such cooperation to the participants play an important role in creating an appropriate climate in which agreements can be worked out. Such studies should be promoted;

c) International finance provided for compensatory schemes can help greatly in promoting cooperative development of international rivers. Such finance should be made available;

   d) Studies should be commissioned to measure and record the quantity of primary renewable energy in the developing countries. Funds should be made available to strengthen the ability of institutions in the developing countries to conduct such studies;

   e) Studies should be commissioned to examine the possibilities of such sources as ethanol, methane and methanol and to assess the extent to which such solutions may be appropriate and feasible for widespread application.

8. THE CONTENT OF DEVELOPMENT

   Growth of GNP is not the whole of development. Development also requires technological and analytical self-reliance. Only a country self-reliant in this way has the power of self-generated development and can hope to stay developed. Development must also include distribution of income and of economic and social power so that at least the basic needs of the poorest people are met; otherwise political instability is likely to result.

Actions:

   a) Institutions in the LDCs should be assisted to develop so that such countries may become more self-reliant;

   b) Education and training in skills relevant to developing countries need to be promoted. This can be done through programs and projects that are carried out jointly by economic scientists from various countries. These projects may be of technical R & D type as well as for the development of skills;

   c) Although the distribution of power and income in any country is a matter of domestic policies, redistribution efforts are always painful and costly. Outsiders can help by providing the resources needed to make such redistribution programs possible.

9. INTERNATIONAL ORGANIZATION IN THE ENERGY AREA

   A number of international organizations operate, each with only a specialized mandate, in the energy area. These are the International Atomic Energy Agency, the International Energy Agency, OLADE, OAPEC and OPEC. The first is open to global membership but restricted to dealing with atomic energy. The others have membership restricted to regional or functional groupings.

   A number of functions are not now covered by these organizations:

   • There is no multinational body concerned with oil supply security for oil importers of the developing countries. IEA covers the subject for its 18 members.

- There is no international agency that focuses on financing energy development within developing countries. In the case of food a special fund has been created. From time to time people have proposed similar special funds for energy development including petroleum development and in some formulations renewable energy development.
- There is no international custodian of information on development of energy (the FAO, for example, performs this service in the world of food), and no global institution to undertake global energy analyses.
- There is no global forum where developing countries' views on energy can be heard (the World Food Council serves this purpose in the world of food).
- There is no international agency to promote renewable energy in developing countries or to goad the industrial countries to do more research applicable to the needs of developing countries.

Actions:

There was no consensus at the Cairo workshop on whether a new international energy agency is needed to cover these functions or whether they might better be tackled *ad hoc* by existing public and non-governmental agencies.

It was agreed that these topics need further discussion in all appropriate forums, private and public. The topics also need further scholarly work, especially work involving specialists from developing countries.

CHAPTER THREE

Protecting Developing Nation Oil Imports in Periods of Acute Scarcity

HARLAN CLEVELAND

I

The oil importing developing countries utilize, as a group, less than 10 percent (3 million barrels a day) of the effective demand for imported oil. The international flows of energy have been driven by the requirements of the industrial countries and the politico-economic decisions of a few big producers. The oil importing developing countries are, as a group, essentially unrepresented in decisions about the price and supply of oil and gas. The big net producers are organized in the Organization of Petroleum Exporting Countries (OPEC), the big net consumers are organized in the International Energy Agency (IEA), and the rest are not effectively organized at all.

The turn of events in Iran, and a series of decisions by OPEC and by individual OPEC countries, promised in the spring of 1979 to create a scarcity in the world oil market. This will, if nothing is done, bear most heavily on the economic growth of the developing countries that most heavily depend on imported oil. If the global rationing of oil and gas is left entirely to the price system, the most impecunious nations will naturally be left at the end of the queue.

Participants in the Cairo workshop on "Energy Futures of Developing Countries" seemed to agree that non-governmental analysis, proposals and international dialogue would have to precede any formal negotiations

13

among governments to tackle this and other policy problems. In this spirit the Aspen Institute presents these proposals for a system to assure fair access by all to the available supplies of oil in international trade.

II

A "fair access" system would have to contain the following elements:

1. The emergency procedures outlined below would be triggered if world oil supplies available for international trade fall below an agreed figure, expressed in million barrels per day (MBD). This "trigger number" would be set, and revised from year to year as necessary, by an international process that cuts the OIDCs in on the decision.

(The "trigger number" would have to be well short of the IEA "trigger"—defined as the moment when oil supplies fall below 7 percent of a complexly calculated base consumption figure. The IEA norm left room for some squeezing of consumption in the industrial democracies before international allocations and redistributions would become necessary. But most developing countries are closer to the margin, and the moment when special measures come into effect should therefore be earlier. It may even be appropriate to work out an agreement that up to some designated proportion of oil consumption the industrial countries should take on the whole obligation to conserve energy, and only after that point the oil importing developing countries should begin sharing the pinch.);

2. The "essential requirements" of the oil importing developing countries would have to be determined, again by an international process in which OIDCs participate along with members of OPEC and IEA. And again the determination of this important number, expressed in million barrels of oil per day, would have to be revised from year to year as the developing countries advance their economies, find and exploit their indigenous energy resources and increase or cut back their requirements for oil in accordance with their own development strategies.

Once these crucial determinations have been made, there is something for everybody to do:

3. The Organization of Petroleum Exporting Countries would have to consider whether to increase the supply in order to obviate the emergency. If OPEC does not do so, it would arrange to earmark a given percent of its current production, for a finite length of time, for purchase by OIDCs only;

4. The international oil companies, whether private multinational corporations or government-owned companies, would undertake (voluntarily or under the suasion of their home governments) to deliver the earmarked quantities to OIDCs without hiking the price or favoring the highest bidders. (Emergency diversions might justify some minor sur-

charges to reflect the cost of changing existing oil flows in midstream.);

5. The industrial oil-consuming countries, presumably cooperating through IEA, would have to exercise sufficient restraint in the world oil market to leave room for the earmarking of the small but critical supplies to meet the OIDCs' "essential requirements." Such cooperation is the *raison d'être* of the IEA anyway—except that assuring fair access to OIDCs has not been among its purposes.

6. Even with the earmarking of some fraction of world oil supplies for the OIDCs' "essential requirements," some of the developing countries may find it difficult or impossible to buy the earmarked oil. To overcome this problem, and during the emergency only, special credits should be created in the form of Special Drawing Rights (SDRs) and made available by formula to OIDCs to be used for the importation of essential energy by developing countries. The distribution formula would have to be internationally agreed; but in this case the primary responsibility for developing the formula could be left to the OIDCs as a group—in the manner pioneered by the Marshall Plan a generation ago. (If SDRs were being created anyway for monetary reasons, that is to overcome a liquidity shortage, some of the SDRs could be cycled into the system through OIDCs, by designating them to pay for earmarked oil during the period of emergency. If the period happens to be one in which the world liquidity situation does not justify the creation of SDRs on monetary grounds, the creation of the small amounts of SDRs to pay for oil imports by developing countries could be offset by cooperation among the main monetary powers. They could adjust their decisions about the level of the money supply to make sure that the creation of these special SDRs did not in itself add to inflationary pressures in an already too inflationary world.)

III

The scheme outlined above requires comparatively few decisions that would have to be the subject of broad international agreement: setting the "trigger figure" that turns on the emergency procedures, determining the quantities of oil imports that constitute "essential requirements," and creating SDRs to pay for oil imports in a pinch. Agreement on the SDR-creation formula could be sought through the machinery of the International Monetary Fund—with a special procedure for letting OIDCs develop a mutually agreeable formula for distribution of any SDRs created for this special purpose. Other decisions required—by OPEC to earmark oil for the OIDCs; by the home governments of the multinational oil companies to induce them to cooperate in the plan; by the industrial democracies (the Soviet Union and its friends would probably sit out this dance, as they have been regularly doing on "North-South" economic issues) to constrain their own oil imports by cooperating through IEA—could be arrived at through the use of existing machinery (OPEC, IEA, and the regular communication between home governments and multinationals in the energy field).

For the decisions requiring broad agreement, the usual dilemma would have to be faced squarely: how to cut everybody in on the decision and still get something done? There are, however, a number of international functions that have been successfully performed by relying on an international executive directly supervised by a governing board of reasonable size, containing representatives of differing groups or regions. These operating boards often have an obligation, in turn, to consult with a wider circle of nations, even with all the members of the United Nations through the General Assembly. INTELSAT, the Global Atmospheric Research Project and the World Bank with its regional executive directors are three examples of the principle at work in different practical situations.

Another model is the "extranational institution," in which a collective executive (such as the European Commission) is appointed by individual governments but cannot be removed by them, and to which nations are willing to delegate the taking of policy initiatives within a prescribed category of subject matter (in the Treaty of Rome analogy, "European" questions). To negotiate such a system for a problem with a global reach would take too long and get too complicated for the management of emergency procedures of the kind outlined above. But it would be worth considering for longer-range international functions in the energy field— the management of a special petroleum reserve, arranging for expeditious exploration of indigenous energy resources in the OIDCs, sponsoring research-and-development activities of special relevance to the OIDCs, working on the special problems of rural energy demand and supply, and providing an authoritative and reasonable independent source of facts, statistics and analysis of energy issues touching the interests of the OIDCs.

Meanwhile, the urgent need for emergency procedures leads us to a less complicated and far-reaching institutional proposal: that representatives of IEA, OPEC, and the OIDCs form a "consortium of the concerned" to establish the "trigger figure" (i.e., answer the question: When is a shortage an emergency?), agree on a system for establishing and revising a determination of "essential requirements" for oil imports by the OIDCs and monitor the actions of all concerned (OPEC countries, IEA countries, OIDCs and the international oil industry) to make sure they are acting in ways consistent with the basic purpose of these arrangements: to assure fair access by oil importing developing countries to supplies of imported oil during periods of acute shortage. The "consortium of the concerned" might, for example, include five members of IEA, five members of OPEC, nine nations acting on behalf of the OIDCs, and one representative of those developing countries which are net exporters of petroleum yet not members of OPEC.* Representation might be rotated to some extent, but it would be advisable to assure that the biggest supplier and the biggest importer (Saudi Arabia and the United States) are always members.

This consortium, acting by consensus, not by voting, would appoint an international executive to develop the necessary analytical staff and set up arrangements to monitor world energy flows, growth patterns in the developing countries and other considerations required to make (and from time to time revise) the necessary determinations and alert the consortium members to problems and failure to cooperate on the part of any element in the complex system. So much analytical work is now being done in so many organizations concerned with world energy issues and with international development that it should not be necessary to generate a large international bureaucracy or sponsor much original research. (A special effort on rural energy supply and demand might be an exception to this rule.)

The consortium, in turn, would report to and consult with a "circle of the consulted," which could either be an existing global assembly (Committee 2 of the General Assembly, or the Economic and Social Council of the United Nations), or an *ad hoc* global assembly on the model of INTELSAT, or even a periodic conference convened by the consortium itself. Whatever "circle of the consulted" is used or formed, the important thing is that in enabling those to act who have the capacity to act, the actors have an obligation to subject their actions to the open scrutiny of those whose interests are affected by their actions.

IV

How could such a system get off the drawing board and into the realm of practical action? The United States government, which has special obligations as the largest oil importer, could well float such a proposal after due consultation with a representative group of the prospective "actors," including not only governments but leaders of the international oil industry.

Meanwhile, to prepare the way and test the water, the Aspen Institute will be discussing the outlines of this suggestion through nongovernmental channels in the United States and abroad.

---

*Angola, Bahrein, Bolivia, Brunei, Congo, Egypt, Malaysia, Mexico, Oman, Syria, Trinidad and Tobago, Tunisia and Zaire.

CHAPTER FOUR

South-North Cooperation
on Energy for Development

JAMES W. HOWE WITH JAMES J. TARRANT III
AND JULIE A. MARTIN

PART I: ENERGY AND DEVELOPMENT

A. THE LINK BETWEEN ENERGY AND DEVELOPMENT

Material progress is dependent upon the use on energy. Capturing and utilizing different energy sources—-animate and inanimate—to substitute for human labor and enable man to increase his natural productivity has been a dominant theme of economic development for most of history. The first major breakthrough, the agricultural revolution 10,000 years ago, consisted of domesticating animals and plants and freed the human population from the onerous process of hunting and gathering. The dawn of the Industrial Revolution around 1750 started the process of harnessing great amounts of inanimate energy to enhance and save human physical labor. The advent of the computer age in this century has improved greatly the productivity of human mental labor. New forms of energy and more efficient ways of using existing energy forms have also yielded a greater and better quality output than previous technology. In essence, human material well-being has come to allow for a relatively more satisfying life through the use of better tools and the substitution of non-human energy for human energy.

Professor Marion J. Levy defines modernization in terms of using "inanimate sources of power and... tools to multiply the effect of effort."[1] In a similar vein, Harrison Brown contends that "the concepts of civilization and the controlled use of energy are inseparable."[2] In order to provide for the material development of the world's people, a great deal of energy must substitute for or supplement human muscle power. Without adequate amounts of non-human energy in usable forms and at affordable prices, there is little prospect of improving the world's currently poor capability of meeting basic human needs for food, water, shelter, clothing, health, employment and education.

There is no perfect correlation between the quantity of energy used and human well-being. It is possible for a nation to use a great deal of energy without improving the human condition very much; and, conversely, it is possible to make significant improvements in human welfare under conditions of relatively low modern energy consumption. The latter is illustrated by four countries: Sri Lanka, Paraguay, Costa Rica and Grenada. In each of these the Physical Quality of Life Index (a composite of infant mortality, life expectancy at age one, and literacy) is relatively high.[3] Yet all of these countries use relatively little commercial energy on a per capita basis, especially compared to more energy-intensive, "advanced" developing countries. It seems likely that the efficient organization and provision of basic needs services at the local level can enhance the productivity of the energy allocated to meeting those needs.

Before we go further, the term energy needs to be defined. As used in the North and by most energy analysts throughout the world, it is understood to include only energy that is bought and sold in markets where it enters into national accounts. In practice, this limits "energy" largely to oil, gas, coal and electricity from any source. Thus, for example in the United States, oil is estimated to supply about 45 percent of all energy. In the developing market economies, on the average, it officially counts for 63 percent of all "energy" (i.e., commercial energy).[4]

The latter figure is, in reality, only the visible tip of what is an energy iceberg. Firewood, animal draft power and other traditional energy sources are no longer of much significance in most industrialized countries, but they are still important in most developing countries. Since they are largely non-commercial sources (i.e., they are usually utilized by the person who finds them; or, if sold in a market, the transaction is not recorded for national accounts), they are generally ignored and their importance grossly underestimated.

India, which has relatively good data, serves as a useful illustration of the importance of non-commercial energy. When only commercial sources are included (i.e., fossil fuels, hydro and nuclear power), India's total energy use is 129.9 million metric tons of coal equivalent (tce). Inclusion of non-commercial energy (e.g., wood fuel, crop residues and dung) more than doubles the total to 309.3 million tce. A still more accurate picture is obtained by including animal draft power, which adds one-fourth more energy, raising the total to 387.1 million tce. If the conventional definition of energy is used, oil, gas, coal and electricity supply all of India's energy. But, in fact, these sources only supply one-third of India's total energy. If human labor were included, commercial energy's share would drop even further.[5]

Clearly, any analysis of India's energy situation which includes only conventional energy omits a large fraction of the total consumption. And in some countries, the ratio of non-commercial to commercial fuels may be as high as nine to one.[6] The substantial contribution of non-commercial energy to most developing country economies must be recognized in the development of any comprehensive energy policy.

While non-commercial energy continues to dominate the rural areas and urban slums, oil has become the predominant source for the modern sector of developing countries. In such sectors, dependence on this source is often greater than in the United States. But oil has not yet penetrated deeply beyond the modern sector of most Third World countries.

When the industrialized countries were at a stage of their development similar to the Third World today, coal was quickly supplanting wood as the dominant fuel. Eventually coal, in turn, gave way to oil. One major advantage of oil—its low (even declining) price—contributed substantially to Northern development. Unfortunately, while the Third World began its modernization process during the cheap oil era, now that it is moving into modern industry on a greater scale, it cannot look forward to the same cheap energy that the North enjoyed.

In the longer term (if countries living so precariously in the immediate present can find consolation in the longer term) this lower dependence on oil (except for the nascent Third World modern sector) may end up sparing many Third World countries some of the difficulty of shifting to other sources as supplies of oil and gas decline and prices rise.

B. CITIES AND FACTORIES:
WHERE MOST OF THE ENERGY GOES

The present explosive population growth within the developing countries may lead to an increase of as much as 1.3 billion people between now and the year 2000. Almost three-fourths of this number will be absorbed by cities.[7] Presently, about 25 percent of the people in Africa and South Asia, 30-40 percent of those in East Asia and North Africa and nearly 60 percent of Central and South Americans live in urban areas.[8] To meet industrial, commercial and residential needs, large energy systems are being developed. These usually take the form of central power stations with extensive transmission and distribution facilities and improved transportation networks. But, even these grids are proving inadequate as demand grows. In fact, with urban populations doubling every 10-15 years, many conurbations in developing countries are already suffering from "systems-overload."[9]

The postwar era of cheap oil facilitated the beginnings of a transition from traditional fuels to commercial energy in developing countries which has contributed to more than an eightfold increase in the consumption of oil over the past quarter century.[10] Central to this expansion has been increasing industrialization and concurrent infrastructure development, particularly in the more advanced developing countries. Globally, modern industry and modern transportation have evolved primarily oil-based technologies, a reflection of the fact that these two sectors grew tremendously in the North during the postwar era of cheap petroleum. Not unexpectedly, oil has dominated these sectors in the South also.

There are several levels of energy-use within the cities of the developing countries. The major consumer of conventional fuels is the *formal sector,* which includes modern industry, commercial establishments and government enterprises. The *informal sector,* comprising small business and a vast array of services characteristic of most Third World cities, utilizes both traditional and conventional fuels. The same is true of the transportation sector. Finally, *slum dwellers and squatters,* often a majority of a city's inhabitants, use a wide variety of energy sources, although the proportion of traditional energy they utilize is usually greater than in the other urban sectors.

The Formal Sector

Productive enterprises in the formal sector are both capital and energy intensive compared with the rest of the economy, are heavily influenced by government regulation and operate on a large scale.[11] Commercial energy is frequently used for building the physical plant, and in the production, transportation and marketing of various manufactured goods.

Many developing countries have embarked on development strategies that call for expansion of the formal sector, especially of their industrial capacity. Reasons for this include import substitution policies, employment absorption and, especially, the desire to capture a greater portion of the value added through processing and manufacturing of goods for export to the developed countries.

To accomplish this goal, more sophisticated industrial technology needs to be used in developing countries, much of which is very energy-intensive (especially in basic materials production like steel-making, oil refining, etc.). Moreover, most research and development on new technologies is being done outside the developing countries with little concern for adapting technologies or substituting indigenous fuels to fit the infrastructural problems or development strategy of these countries. As a result, urban areas, especially in the middle level countries with important industrialized and modern commercial sectors, have tended to use a growing and disproportionate share (on a per capita basis) of national commercial energy consumption. For the oil importing developing countries (OIDCs) since 1973, the price of this oil dependency has been high in terms of foreign exchange expenditures and an inability to absorb the unemployed.

In some countries, policies have been introduced to try to prevent modern energy use from increasing unemployment. Some of these policies have made better use of local-factor endowments than has previously been the case, and one of their collateral results has also been a saving of commercial fuels. For example, the Indian hand spindle, although requiring greater capital per unit of output than modern power looms, employs much more labor, saves commercial energy and distributes income broadly.[12] The plywood industries of South Korea have taken advantage of their relatively lower labor costs to show that varying factor combinations can be used to perform the same task with more labor and less capital than in the U.S. and at an overall lower cost (although low labor costs alone cannot justify the use of a technology over the long term).[13]

In a number of industries in the North, improvements have been made in reduction techniques, preheaters, cogeneration cycles, energy conscious maintenance and the use of substitute fuels. All of these efforts have greatly reduced commercial energy requirements.[14] However, many of these technologies are not yet employed in the developing countries.

The urban formal sector also encompasses energy used for electricity, lighting, heating and cooling in commercial establishments and government offices. In many instances, more attention to efficiency, conservation and development of appropriate materials, design and insulation could lower the high energy cost of operating these facilities. In the case of electricity supplies, this rapid formal-sector growth in demand has often outstripped supply or prevented the extension of electricity to the large numbers of people flooding into the cities. Increasingly, demand is requiring huge investments for these economies. South Korea, for example, with electricity consumption bounding upward at a 20 percent rate of annual increase, has revised its nuclear power projections recently, claiming that it will need 43 reactor stations by the year 2000 to meet modern energy needs. At this level, Korea would have almost two-thirds as many nuclear power stations as the U.S. now has.[15]

The Informal Sector

Labor-intensive services have traditionally accounted for a large proportion of employment in urban areas. These traditional or technologically hybrid aspects of the urban economy are collectively referred to as "informal sector" activities. They have provided important links between modern and traditional culture, as well as the integration of commercial and non-commercial energy use.

The informal sector is characterized by self-employment, irregular hours, erratic work conditions, small-scale labor intensive production and relatively greater labor mobility.[16] In many developing countries these small industries and repair services provide low cost goods needed by the formal sector. The inability of many cities to absorb surplus labor into the formal work force has resulted in large, and often increasing, informal-sector employment and underemployment. Estimates of the proportion of total employees working in this sector range as high, for example, as 69 percent in Belo Horizonte, Brazil, and 53 percent in Lima.[17] Three-quarters of those employed in the manufacturing sectors of India, Sri Lanka, Thailand and the Philippines work in small-scale informal enter-prises with 20 or fewer workers.[18]

Informal sector workers fall roughly into three categories: (1) "back-yard" producers, (2) domestic employees and (3) self-employed street vendors and service providers.

The backyard producers maintain a symbiotic relationship between the formal and informal sectors through the exchange of raw materials, energy, repairs and intermediate technology. For example, an urban building project may use modern earth-moving equipment, bricks pro-duced by a small backyard kiln and day-laborers contracted from the city's slums. The importance of the backyard sector lies in the provision of useful goods at affordable prices, relying on mostly traditional fuels, using li-mited amounts of modern commercial energy and recycling the products of the modern sector.[19]

Domestic servants, the majority of whom are women, make up a sig-nificant portion of service sector employment. Their labor often is used in place of modern energy-intensive appliances; they perform tasks made unnecessary in the North by the abundance of labor-saving conveniences. In the South, these tasks sometimes include shopping several times a day because of a lack of refrigeration, tending fires, hand washing, drying and ironing clothes and cleaning house.

The range of self-employed services exemplifies the ingenuity of the informal sector workers in inventing employment opportinities. Such services employ food vendors, unofficial health and education workers, rickshaw drivers, and street corner barkers.

Commercial energy consumption would rise significantly if informal sector services utilized modern energy sources and discarded the valuable practice of recycling materials, as happens in the North; or if the modern sector increased its use of modern high energy appliances in place of servants.

Slums and Squatter Sections
    While city populations are often growing at 3-10 percent per year—twice the average national rate (a result of migration and natural increase)—the slum and squatter sections are typically growing at two or three times the rate of the city as a whole.[20] The sometimes illegal and

often unserviced slum sections may contain up to 90 percent of a city's population. [21] The World Bank estimates that almost one-third of urban dwellers in developing countries—most of whom depend upon the informal sector for employment—lack incomes sufficient to maintain a productive life. Based on estimates that more than 250 million urban dwellers currently lack access to basic human requirements, such as safe water, minimal nutrition, sanitation, shelter and basic education, the World Bank predicts that by the end of the century 600 million people will face similar circumstances. [22] Rapid growth of population and migration have made it difficult for many cities to supply even basic services at a rate sufficient to meet the needs of their people.

Shelter, a fundamental human need requiring energy, is often inadequate. Building materials either recycled or made in small local industries frequently deteriorate rapidly. More permanent structures are frequently costly and require relatively large amounts of energy to make the materials and operate construction equipment. Hybrid styles, incorporating rural and modern elements, are common. Apart from these fixed inputs in construction, there is also an energy requirement for maintenance and utilities.

The provision of municipal services also requires energy. For example, clean water, essential for health, requires pumping energy. The World Health Organization estimated that 50 percent of urban dwellers have no regular water supply and 26 percent have access only to public standpipes. [23] To meet their water needs would require significant financial and energy investments in pumping, sewage and treatment facilities.

Fuel for cooking is the major domestic energy need in the slums. With the oil price rise, many people have been forced to lessen or discontinue the use of bottled gas and kerosene as a cooking fuel and turn to firewood and charcoal. This has increased pressure on forests around metropolitan areas, leading to serious deforestation in many places and subsequently increased wood prices. [24]

Slums are usually the last areas of a city to be electrified. Lighting, radios, TVs and other conveniences, all requiring electricity, are popular demands. Bathing and laundry, now done without the aid of electrical appliances, usually entail some form of solar energy. Extension of electricity and services to large numbers of people in slums and squatter areas would substantially increase energy demands on the cities.

Transportation

An efficient transport sector is vital to the functioning of urban areas. In many cities of the North, roads, railways and ports facilitate the flow of goods and services, while mass transit systems enable workers to commute to places of employment. In contrast, in many cities of the South,

inadequate transport inhibits the full use of human and material resources. Poor urban planning—the relationship of the location of jobs,
schools, stores and houses—complicates transportation in both developed and developing countries.

Most cities of the South depend on a variety of transportation forms,
which include walking, bicycles, horses, carts, motorcycles and automobiles. Public transport includes buses, taxis, jitneys, rickshaws and
pedicabs.

Many transportation systems have emerged in a haphazard manner.
Physical inaccessibility of urban slums to any kind of efficient mass or
freight transport, the high costs of motorized transport and sometimes the
unreliability of services are all impediments to serving the majority of
residents, especially workers living in peripheral slum areas. With the
increases in the physical size of cities, walking is extremely difficult when
time en route reaches 2-3 hours each way.[25]

The number of cars, while increasing, remains relatively small and
limited primarily to the upper classes and public or commercial use. Increased road traffic also means more congestion, pollution and dust. Au-
tomotive transport requires adequate roads; but in many countries, roads
are not paved and may be impassable during the rainy season, especially
in rural areas and urban slums. All-weather roads and petrol for trucks are
essential for trade between rural and urban areas. Energy is also required
to build roads, manufacture transport vehicles and keep them running.

Even excluding other aspects of energy use in the developing world,
transportation requirements can be a significant drain on national
budgets. For the oil importing developing countries, scarce foreign exchange must be used to purchase fuel for transportation systems. On the
other hand, for most developing countries, widespread road transport
systems are vital for internal commerce, communications and security.
Since there is little medium-term likelihood of finding a widespread alternative to the petrol-powered engine, the use of oil for transport will remain high and, in fact, grow much larger.

C. RURAL ENERGY NEEDS:
THE NEGLECTED PART OF DEVELOPMENT

The Scope of the Rural Energy Problem

During the past generation, the developing countries have labored to
improve their standard of living. Following the model of the Northern
nations, the thrust of this effort has gone primarily toward the urban and
industrial parts of the nation. Yet, in the overwhelming majority of these
countries, most of the people live in rural areas, engaged primarily in
subsistence farming.

The size of the rural sector is staggering: probably as many as 2.2 billion people in all the developing countries or well over half the world's population. Regionally, the rural population ranges as high as 80 percent in Oceania to about 39 percent in Latin America. But the vast bulk of the rural population lives in the developing countries of Asia and Africa, each of which is only about one-quarter urbanized.[26]

The energy significance of these figures lies not so much in their absolute amounts as in the changes occurring within the rural sector—changes which, because of the size of the population involved, could exert a potentially enormous cumulative impact on the international energy balance. Most rural people live in relatively dispersed—and poor—agriculturally based settlements. The chief characteristic of these is the predominant use of human and animal energy in farming and traditional, non-commercial fuels in most other activities.

A combination of forces is now working to cause changes in this relatively neglected area. The concentration of attention on developing a modern industrialized and service sector in many countries often means that scarce capital and manpower cannot be allocated to rural areas. The continuing post-independence tide of urban migration is a reflection of the neglect of the rural areas and the attraction of possibly more and better jobs and a higher standard of living to be found in the cities. Many developing countries actually face food shortages exacerbated by this past rural neglect and the need to feed large urban populations.

Today, domestic and foreign assistance development programs are being targeted toward improving the subsistence sector. But, if past experience in the North and the more recent experience of the "Green Revolution" in Asia are indications, improving agriculture and rural life is going to require, among other things, a significantly greater expenditure of inanimate energy. In terms of direct use, modern forms of energy will be needed for more intensive cultivation and irrigation, as well as for processing and transporting of crops. Indirectly, modern energy finds its way into high quality fertilizers, and food preservation and storage. Modern energy is also increasingly required to cook food where traditional energy supplies are inadequate. At present, modern commercial energy use is meager in rural areas. Petroleum-based fuels are the most immediately applicable conventional energy sources for the two principal rural problems, motive power and cooking. But, aside from long-term supply limitations, petroleum products must be imported in many countries. In the following section, we will briefly elaborate on the critical rural energy problems facing developing countries.

Rural Energy Use: The Unseen Energy Crisis

Most of the energy used in rural areas comes from traditional sources.

If one looks at a village in India from the point of view of conventional energy alone (e.g., oil, gas, coal, and electricity), consumption is only about 750 kilocalories per capita per day. With the inclusion of traditional energy, this figure rises to 7000 kilocalories.[27] India is a useful developing country example in this case, not only because of the sheer size of its rural population—at 501 millions, it is larger than the combined rural populations of Africa and Latin America[28]—but also because it is in a transitional stage similar to that of many Asian, African and Latin American states. Most of the energy consumed in rural areas goes to cooking and agriculture. Food preparation, in fact, consumes more energy than any other village task. Pimental estimates that 60-80 percent of energy used in a village is for meeting food needs and that about 60 percent of this amount is required for cooking.[29] Human labor is necessary for growing crops, pounding grain, carrying water for cooking and other food processing or preserving tasks. In many societies, a few individuals in each family spend several days per week gathering firewood for cooking fires. Women, in particular, are almost always burdened with the task of finding sufficient fuel. Women and children in the foothills of Nepal hike miles to gather firewood and fodder, a task sometimes requiring entire days. Only a generation ago, this job required no more than an hour or two of work. With increasing scarcities of these fuels, live tree branches, shrubs, seedlings and grasses are consumed after harvests to use as fuel.[30] In some areas, the consequences of this are expanding deforestation and even devegetation. Soil erosion increases and leads to lowered crop productivity and silting of dams. The unchecked run-off of water results in flooding. In some areas, where wood or charcoal are marketed, as much as 30 percent of a family's budget may be required for cooking fuel.[31] The rise in world oil prices has increased demand for wood and charcoal as substitutes for kerosene. This intensifies the problem.[32]

A.K.N. Reddy estimates that Indian agriculture requires about 55 percent of the human labor expended in daily village activity and about 84 percent of the available bullock work potential. Together, these sources comprise 90 percent of total energy used in agriculture.[33]

Crop Production

Preparation of agricultural land (plowing, planting, weeding and cultivating) is today done mostly with human or animal muscles. In many developing regions, increased irrigation is necessary to yield sufficient crop production to meet the growing need for food, especially where there are seasonal and erratic rainfall patterns. Human and animal powered pumps often do not yield enough water for irrigation because water tables are frequently deep. Significant increases in irrigation will, in many cases, require some sort of inanimate energy to pump water a substantial distance or height.[34]

In many places, increased irrigation will not be effective without proper drainage systems. Building necessary drainage ditches, many of which must be cement, tile or plastic-lined to prevent too much water seepage, requires energy.

Harvesting and processing (e.g., cutting and threshing, husking, shucking, shelling, crushing and grinding) require intensive energy. Most of the tasks are now performed by humans or animals with crude implements. The bottlenecks that frequently occur in this part of the crop cycle can only be overcome with substitutes for human energy or methods of making it more efficient.

Some use is already made of renewable energy sources. Solar energy is important in crop drying, and heating and wind may be used to separate grain from chaff.

Marketing

Marketing of crops takes energy. Food is transported to market towns by horses, mules or donkey and ox carts. In many places, people alone transport their market goods. To a lesser extent, buses and trucks are used. Once food reaches a market town, it may be transported to urban centers by trucks; but the initial dependence on human and animal transport has severely limited internal trade in many countries.

Social Welfare

This cycle of poor energy use affects the quality of life in rural areas. Education, for example, is impaired by a lack of energy. Children are essential parts of the energy budgets and the work schedules in developing countries, particularly during heavy labor demand periods in the crop cycle. Often, children cannot be spared from household maintenance needs (for firewood and water especially) and farm production to attend school full time.[35] Darkness at the day's end further hampers study.

Inhabitants of rural areas often lack many basic human needs. Electricity is vital for decent lighting, water pumping, refrigeration and other amenities such as radios.

In 1971, the percentages of village rural population served by electricity were Latin America, 23 percent; North Africa and the Middle East, 15 percent; Asia, 16 percent; and Africa, 4 percent. Given the present rate of expansion of about 1 percent per year, only one in four rural inhabitants will live in areas with electricity by the year 2000; and unless incomes increase, electricity still will not be affordable for even the majority of those living in electrified areas by that time.[36]

The Traditional Energy Solution

A great deal of village farming continues to be low in output, and efforts to improve productivity are going to require more and better energy. If acreage is expanded, more labor (whether human, animal or mechanical) will be needed. If more intensive cultivation is sought, energy will be needed to drive irrigation pumps or to make high quality fertilizers and other chemicals.

The predominant use of non-commercial energy poses a dilemma to increasing agricultural productivity. Increasing the traditional inputs— land, labor and draft animal power—without increasing their productivity may worsen the problem. In order to farm marginal land, trees may have to be cut down or pasture converted to crop land. There will be a loss of both fuel wood and forage for animals, leaving the farmer short of fuel to cook with and short of animal draft power to farm the new land.

In any event, the added production from such marginal lands may be meager. The loss of forest and pastures ensures that more soil will be lost, and the loss of dung deprives the remaining soil of nutrients. Increasing human energy at present productivity levels may not provide the solution either. More labor merely means more population pressure, which in many rural areas is already substantial, and contributes to demand for food and fuel. Adding animal traction will not be possible where land is scarce, since each animal requires land for fodder. In short, the problem of increasing food production by means of traditional sources is often self-defeating. More modern or improved energy sources and conversion will be needed.

Traditional sources of soil enrichment—crop residues and dung—are limited by added demands for energy for cooking fuels. When dung cakes are burned, agricultural production suffers because of reduced fertilizer for soil enrichment. And with high oil prices, petroleum-based fertilizers remain unaffordable to the masses. In such circumstances, reliance on non-commercial energy becomes a trade-off between maintaining soil fertility and meeting energy needs for cooking.

If all labor and energy inputs into crop production are considered, developing countries are more energy intensive than the highly mechanized countries. [37] However, developing countries are much less fossil fuel intensive, which implies that agricultural modernization along developed country lines would entail high cost in petroleum and energy for tractors, other farm equipment, fertilizer, chemical pesticides, etc. But without some kind of modernization, productivity will remain low and the demand for food will outstrip the supply. The consequences include malnutrition and low work efficiency, which in turn lead to lower food production, continuing a vicious cycle.

The absence of some kind of modern power will mean that rural industries and service will be inhibited. The effect will be to increase the disparity between city and countryside with detrimental effects on both areas. However, a massive switch to modern energy is also inhibited by cultural factors. For example, replacement of bullocks with tractors would affect other aspects of rural life. Draft animals are a source of beef, milk, dung and transportation services vital to a functioning household. Similarly, open wood fires, though low in efficiency, may serve as sources of warmth or play a ritual and cultural role. [38]

The problems outlined above require early solutions that cannot be provided by traditional energy alone. Present development strategies, growing population and expectations for higher standards of living are putting demands upon agricultural systems that cannot be met. Part of the problem is not energy-related. The need for land reform, unresponsive educational or governmental institutions or the existence of political crises may be preventing needed changes in the countryside. But, as we have noted, energy use is a fundamental aspect of development, and a large part of the solutions to the rural sector's problems will involve increasing energy supplies.

The two principal rural energy problems—a lack of sufficient motive power and efficient cooking fuels—are mainly the result of the inadequacies of human and animal labor, the growing scarcity of noncommercial fuels and the inefficiency of the traditional technologies that are used with them.

We turn now to a discussion of conventional rural energy alternatives, most of which have been oil-based.

The Conventional Energy Solution

The conventional energy solution for motive power has favored the use of tractors, tillers and harvesters powered by petroleum-based fuels. It has emphasized the need for trucks, buses and smaller vehicles for internal communications, trade, marketing and national unification. Diesel pumps are used for irrigation. For the foreseeable future, oil-powered transportation for most countries will continue to be indispensable.

There is considerable scope for improved productivity and better use of existing resources. In many countries, moreover, the widespread use of oil-powered farm machinery is controversial. Most farms are too small to support individual family tractors in terms of cost-effectiveness per unit of output gained. Tractors have been criticized for distorting rural labor markets for certain crops and for displacing tenant farmers. [39] The cost and reliable supply of oil-based fuels is an increasing problem. Tractors also need careful maintenance and spare parts. To varying degrees, the same sorts of problems occur with conventional tillers, harvesters, crop processing equipment and diesel pumps.

The conventional energy solution for cooking fuels has been the use of kerosene because of its high heat content and convenience. The interaction between kerosene and traditional fuels is a close one. Village and nationwide studies in India, Bangladesh, the Sudan and other places have indicated (a) the vulnerability of kerosene to supply interruptions and (b) the effect of kerosene price increases in pushing up the price of their nearest substitute—the often scarce supplies of wood and charcoal. [40] Following the oil price hike of 1973-74 and the oil embargo, kerosene supplies were interrupted in a number of developing countries. Frequently, the government would divert rural supplies to the cities to prevent urban unrest. This and the rise in the price of kerosene switched fuel demand to increasingly scarce fuel wood and charcoal supplies, which have not been able to satisfy this demand (especially in fragile climate/high population areas). Another possible more technical long-term problem is that kerosene is a high distillate of oil. If a rapid expansion in the demand for kerosene occurs, this could put the production of kerosene in direct competition with production of other high distillates, especially gasoline for transportation, and possibly lead to serious refining bottlenecks. [41]

One of the causes of rural emigration is the availability of electricity in urban areas and market towns. Electricity in rural areas would make possible decent lighting, public services, improved rural industry and commercial employment. In addition, rural people want electricity for specific agricultural tasks such as water pumping for irrigation and the operation of some crop processing equipment. The spread of electrification by conventional means has been very slow in developing countries. The World Bank estimates that only 12 percent of the village-rural populations of these countries have access to electricity. [42] Even for those in the rural areas with access to electricity, the cost of extension lines and rural home hookups is often prohibitive. The village may be initially electrified by placing a diesel generator in the village. Eventually, when electricity is available and the demand for it high enough, the village is integrated into the national grid. The other alternative is direct integration into the grid by extending a sub-transmission line to the village. In both cases, the unsubsidized costs of electrification, if they were borne solely by the village, would usually be prohibitive. Though in remote areas diesel generation costs less than grid supplies, it requires reliable access to often costly and imported diesel fuel and continual expert maintenance and repair of the generator. These factors—combined with the lower rural population densities, lower load factors, and inability to pay for unsubsidized electricity—have greatly inhibited the pace of rural electrification. [43]

D. DEMAND VS. NEEDS:
THE FUTURE ENERGY PICTURE FOR THE THIRD WORLD

1. Energy Demand in the Third World

A number of projections of Third World commercial energy consumption to the year 2000 have been published recently. These are summarized in Table 1 on page 34. A summary of projections of Third World oil consumption is given in Table 2 on page 35.

These studies show estimates of commercial energy consumption in the Third World ranging from 35 to 64 million barrels a day oil equivalent (MBDOE) in the year 2000 and estimates of oil alone ranging from 15 to 24 million barrels a day (MBD). Corresponding figures for the base year (mostly 1975) are about 10 MBDOE (18.5 with centrally planned Asian economies [CPA] included) of commercial energy of which about 8 MBD (9.8 with CPA) is oil. [44] Thus the estimates suggest at least a doubling of oil consumption, using the highest figures, and an increase in total commercial energy use of 2 to 3 times. (The commercial energy figures usually do not include China.) If this increase in oil consumption is actually achieved, it would mean that the Third World would be consuming somewhat more in the year 2000 than the United States in 1979, with total petroleum consumption of about 20 MBD of which nearly half would need to be imported.

2. Estimate of Future Energy Needs

The figures in Tables 1 and 2 estimate likely energy consumption for the year 2000 if supplies are readily available, at prices comparable in magnitude to the present. They do not necessarily show the link between energy supply and development needs. Starting with a calculation of how much energy is required to meet economic growth and basic human needs as enough food, water, shelter, clothing, education, health care and the like, Prasad and Reddy have tried to make such a calculation for India. [45] They use a per capita figure of 28,000 kilocalories (kCal) per day including both non-commercial and commercial energy. This amount of energy would allow the average rural Indian to quintuple his current use of 5600 kCal of energy. This sounds like a large increase, but it would still be very austere by comparison to the current U.S. per capita average of 202,000 kCal per day.

It should be noted that this 28,000 figure is a very rough notion of quantifiable energy needs. In the absence of any multi-country energy needs assessment, it provides an idea of how far most developing countries are from reaching an even minimal energy standard. More detailed study is needed of a minimum acceptable per capita energy consumption figure, particularly in a series of developing country cultural contexts.

TABLE 1

Developing Countries'
Commercial Energy Consumption and Projections
for 1985, 2000

Country Category	Base Year	1985	2000
	(millions of barrels/day of oil equivalent)		
Source of Projection			
Non-OPEC LDCs			
IER[1] (1975)	9.1	—	28.3-41.9
WAES[2] (1972)	9.1	14.9-18.2	26.5-35.6
IEA[3] (1975)	8.9 (1975)	17.5	37.7
OPEC			
WAES	1.7	4.2-4.9	8.4-13.10
IEA	2.1	5.2	14.1
All LDCs			
WAES	10.8	19.1-23.1	34.9-48.7
ODC[4] (1975)	10.5 (1974)	18.5-23.5	41.1-63.6
IEA	11.0	22.7	51.8

SOURCES:

[1]Robert Nathans, with Romir Chatterjee, Manuel Taylor, Arandhati Ghash Dastider, "Energy Demand Projections for the Developing Countries" (Stony Brook, New York: The Institute for Energy Research, March 1978).

[2]Workshop on Alternative Energy Strategies, *Energy, Global Prospects, 1985-2000* (Cambridge, Mass.: MIT Press, 1977.)

[3]International Energy Agency, Standing Group on Long-Term Co-operation, "Technical Report on the Energy Prospects for Developing Countries," Paris, Feb. 1978.

[4]Energy projections of the Overseas Development Council are included in Hamilton-Rabinovitz, Inc., *Alternative Perspectives on the Economic Evolution of Developing Countries:* Final Report, Prepared for the Agency for International Development, Contract No. AID/Otr C-1570 (Los Angeles: Hamilton-Rabinovitz, Inc., Feb. 1978).

TABLE 2

Recent Projections of Developing Countries' Petroleum Consumption

	Base Year	1976	1980	1985	2000
			(millions of barrels/day)		
OPEC					
OECD (1974)[5]	1.9		2.9	4.1-4.2	
CIA[6]		2.1	3.0	4.0	
WAES (1972)				2.8-3.3	3.0-7.8
IEA (1974)	1.2			3.5	6.1
DOE (1975)[7]	1.7			3.0-3.6	4.0-5.3 (1990)
Non-OPEC LDCs					
OECD (1974)	5.0		5.3	6.2	
CIA		6.7	8.5	12.0	
WAES				8.9-10.7	14.6-20.9
CRS (1975)[8]					
IER (1975)	6.9				15.2-21.9
IEA (1975)	5.5			10.6	17.7
DOE (1975)	6.3			11.1-12.7	14.6-16.2 (1990)
All LDCs					
OECD	6.9		8.2	10.3-10.4	
CIA	8.8		11.5	16.0	
WAES				11.7-14	
CRS					
IER	6.9				15.2-21.9
IEA	n.a.			14.1	23.8
DOE (1975)	8.0			14.1-16.3	18.6-21.5 (1990)

SOURCES:

[5]OECD, *World Energy Outlook, A Reassessment of Long-Term Developments and Related Policies* (Paris, 1977).

[6]U.S. Central Intelligence Agency, "The International Energy Situation: Outlook to 1985," Document No. ER 77-10240U, Washington, D.C., April, 1977.

[7]U.S. Dept. of Energy, Energy Information Administration, *Annual Report to Congress, Vol. II, 1977, "Projections of Energy Supply and Demand and Their Impacts,"* DOE/EIA-0036/2, Washington, D.C., April, 1978.

[8]Library of Congress, Congressional Research Service, "Project Independence: U.S. and World Energy Outlook Through 1990," Summary Report to Senate Committees on Energy and Natural Resources and Interstate and Foreign Commerce, Washington, D.C., June, 1977.

Applying this illustrative 28,000 kCal minimum energy needs standard to the expected population of the Third World in the year 2000 yields a "need" for energy of 95 MBDOE.[46] This, of course, includes both commercial and non-commercial energy. Today, the Third World consumes 18.4 MBDOE of commercial energy alone. There are no reliable estimates of how much non-commercial energy is used. It has been estimated that in India non-commercial sources provide about as much energy to total consumption as commercial sources.[47] In Africa, the non-commercial share is probably larger; but in Latin America it is likely to be smaller.

Assuming that the Indian average is close to that of the entire Third World, one can estimate a current Third World non-commercial energy consumption figure of around 18 MBDOE. This amount is not likely to increase during the rest of this century because population increases are forcing forests and pastures into croplands. Firewood and cattle (and cattle dung) resources may, in fact, decline. If they decline only slightly to 15 MBDOE, that figure may be deducted from the 95 MBDOE of total energy to give a commercial energy needs estimate of 80 MBDOE by the year 2000 for the entire Third World. This compares to about 57 MBDOE now being consumed by the entire world.

Once again, it should be pointed out the 80 MBDOE is not an estimate of what is likely to be consumed. It is a calculation of the amount of energy that would be required to meet basic human needs if such could be made available. It is unlikely this target of 28,000 kCal will be achieved by the end of the century. To do so would require that commercial energy consumption, at present efficiencies, be increased well over four times in 22 years. Such a pace is unlikely to be achieved, and hence there will be a gap between what energy is available and the amount needed to reach the target. A failure to meet basic energy needs for these countries is likely to exacerbate many of the socio-economic problems developing countries now face. These include continued low levels of agricultural productivity, which will reduce the chance of meeting minimal food needs; increased migration to cities, where most commercial energy supplies are available; and a stagnation, at the least, in economic development efforts and programs for improving the quality of life in both rural and urban areas.

3. Third World Energy Dilemma

The industrialized countries are forced to make a transition from oil to the sources of energy that will succeed oil. It is a traumatic process, as the first years of the Carter Administration in the United States have demonstrated. The Third World must make the same transition. Insofar as their modern sectors are concerned, they are at least as oil dependent as the industrialized countries; and the transition will be at least as traumatic.

But the Third World has an even more difficult transition to make. This is the transition from traditional energy sources on which most of their people rely to more modern and long lasting sources. They must make this elemental transition for two reasons: First, traditional energy is declining—at least on a per capita, if not on an absolute, basis. Second, even if such energy were plentiful, it is not of good enough quality to permit these countries to achieve their goals for higher incomes, more food, clean drinking water and improved education. This elemental transition to more modern energy is taking place. We are not sure how fast but there is much evidence of the direction: It is nearly always a transition to an oil based technology.

Meanwhile, in the modern sector of the major cities and in the transportation sector of each nation both the pace and the direction of the transition are more certain: Oil consumption in the Third World has increased 829 percent in the third quarter of this century. Even though the initial base was low, this is a spectacular pace and an ominous direction. Clearly, most Third World countries will need to continue to increase their consumption of oil for want of satisfactory and economical alternatives. Meeting the large future urban energy needs in the post oil era will, in part, depend upon technological developments in the North. Here, a major difficulty is likely to be one of scale. If the new technology that emerges from Northern research produces electricity on a gigantic scale only, it will not fit the relatively small grids of the urban-industrial South. Already nuclear fission comes in units too large for the present power grids of most developing countries. If the breeder and, beyond that, fusion are of even larger scale, as appears likely, the needs of the South will not be met by them, until the grids in the South grow much larger.

Fortunately, solar thermal units and photovoltaic cells can be adapted to a wide range of desired scales. Still, neither the breeder reactor nor solar energy currently is able to produce centralized electricity at costs that are competitive with fossil fuels; and it may be a while before they do, even if the price of oil and coal continues to rise. (One significant exception in the area of solar energy is large-scale, centralized hydroelectricity for which there still exists a major potential for development.) In any event, fusion is technologically some distance into the future. For a long interim, the South must depend primarily upon fossil fuels including, for many countries, imported oil to meet centralized urban, industrial and transportation needs. The North is increasingly hesitant about a full-scale commitment to nuclear fission though it retains the option of doing so technically and economically. More importantly, it can rely upon enormous energy savings through conservation to help make the transition to renewable or at least relatively inexhaustible sources. But the South does not have all of these alternatives.

The economies of the North are at a post-industrial stage where they need not increase energy use as rapidly as the Third World. If the South hopes to achieve its internal development goals, its need to increase conventional energy use will be greater than that of the North.

The second Southern problem, the transition by rural areas and urban slums from traditional fuels to a successor is quite different from anything faced by the North. The latter has virtually no rural people without access to electricity, natural gas or other fossil fuels. Because these energy delivery grids already exist in the North, the nearly universal expectation is that the solution to the rural energy needs lies in using them to deliver energy to rural areas from the cities where energy supplies now are concentrated. In the South, few such grids exist. Thus, there is interest in determining whether existing solar technologies, if available in rural areas, could convert the widely dispersed, renewable energy in these areas to a form that would help meet rural energy needs and to do so competitively with conventional energy. If that possibility is real, it would be unfortunate if the Third World ignored it for another decade or two and turned instead to oil. The onset of actual oil shortages together with increasing shortages of traditional energy would force them to begin exploring decentralized renewable energy one or two decades later and put them in deeper trouble than would be the case today.

The direction of the transition toward oil is ominous because global production of oil is likely to peak around the turn of the century and then to begin a long period of decline. Moreover, even though growth in oil consumption in the industrialized countries appears to be levelling off and even declining, demand remains very close to production because of supply limitation imposed by the world's residual oil suppliers, OPEC, to preserve the value of their resources. Even with significant new non-OPEC additions to global oil reserves, it is unlikely that real oil prices will ever go through a progressive decline as they did during the Sixties (a process that distorted energy markets and led to the present crisis). Thus the present is indeed a poor time for the Third World to be acquiring a long-term dependence on oil.

For the immediate future the Third World has no alternative to increased oil use. Few machines on the shelf, that are not oil based, will power certain modern industrial processes. There is little current technology for transportation of persons and goods that does not involve fossil fuel for trucks, buses, trains and automobiles. Even in the countryside, the diesel or gasoline generator and petroleum-fueled lamps and stoves are the easiest to order, the most familiar to maintain and operate, and in many cases the cheapest to install. Any decision to turn away from oil is a decision that will hurt development at least in the short run. The Third World economies are now moving into the energy intensive phase

of producing goods—especially manufactured goods—while the indus-
tialized countries are moving into the less energy intensive post-industrial
phase of producing services.

At the risk of oversimplification, the heart of the dilemma is this: If the
non-oil Third World countries increase their dependence upon oil, they
are storing up trouble for themselves over the next decade or the one
after that. But if they don't use more oil, their development will suffer
immediately.

In these circumstances, it is clear that the Third World will continue to
increase its oil consumption. Though the productivity of this energy can
be improved, one can scarcely foresee a real decline in oil use, given the
lack of competitive alternatives. In the rural sector, it is not clear that oil
based technology is always the most economical and convenient—
especially some distance from the major cities. It may be prudent to speed
up the testing of non-oil based alternatives, including those based on renewable and decentralized energy, and, meanwhile, to make cautiously
any decision toward a major transition to oil in the rural areas. If non-oil
based technology proves to be practical, the delay will have saved capital
and avoided a major false start. If no practical alternative to oil appears, a
course of action will still have to be set to deal with it.

In the modern sector, major increases in oil consumption will be essential, but there should be a conscientious effort to switch to non-oil alternatives just as soon as they appear competitive and not wait until the
industrialized countries have made the transition. In the industrialized
countries, the processes of deciding on energy sources are heavily biased
in favor of oil. Manufacturers, businesses, the residential sector, the oil
industry and the auto industry are locked somewhat inflexibly onto a petroleum course. The vast sums invested in this course and the extraordi-
narily costly process of retrofitting and retrotraining suggest that there will
be a great deal of resistance to the introduction of non-oil investments.

Thus, there may be a long lag between the availability of competitive
non-oil alternatives and their installation in the industrialized countries.
The developing countries may find it possible to avoid this lag and adopt
modern renewable energy technology ahead of the industrialized countries. This would be a welcome reversal of the historical pattern in which
innovations are adopted first in the industrialized countries and only later
tried in the Third World.

PART II: ENERGY TECHNOLOGIES AND STRATEGIES

A. STRATEGIC CHOICES

1. Choice of Development Strategy: Implications for Energy

During the past several decades of intensive nation-building in market and centrally planned economies, three broad developmental trends have emerged. In the first, economic resources tend to go in at the top—to the wealthiest or most powerful groups—and "trickle down" to the rest of the nation. The second attempts to distribute resources widely and "build from the bottom." For most countries, a third trend, which combines these two, has prevailed.

In socio-economic terms, the first development trend has resulted in strategies that emphasize the accumulation of capital, large-scale industrialization, and, in the area of energy, a bias toward labor saving technologies. They have typically led to centralization of economic organization and societal structures; large urban centers are a hallmark of such strategies. The second trend, the intellectual roots of which are based in the ideas of people like Jefferson, Mao and Gandhi, harkens back to the individual or small cooperative group as the focal productive point. It is predominantly rural and, ideally, it seeks to develop an educated or economically cooperative working class. While not anti-technology, it is more inclined to value individual or village self-sufficiency before other political or economic goals.

2. Choice of Energy Strategy

Development strategies strongly influence energy strategies and are affected by them in return. A centralized, large-scale energy strategy tends to fit the "trickle down" development strategy; a decentralized energy strategy tends to fit the "bottom up" development strategy. While oil is adaptable to either energy strategy, most other energy sources appear to be more compatible with one kind of strategy or the other.

Western industrial societies are capital-intensive and urbanized and develop a centralized energy economy capable of supplying large concentrations of inanimate primary and secondary energy to meet their needs. A centralized energy strategy inevitably gives rise to large organizations in charge of regulating the supply and, to some extent, the demand for energy. It also enables the fast and efficient mass production of goods and services.

A decentralized energy strategy, which no society has yet deliberately adopted as its dominant energy pattern, is less well-adapted to large industrial organizations or concentrated urban centers. China, the society that has most deliberately attempted to encourage decentralized energy, has relied heavily on ideologically based communal organizations. As a result, decentralized power sources in China have often been successful and capable of improving production and meeting basic human needs, particularly in rural areas. But how replicable the Chinese experience is to other countries is very uncertain.

Centralized energy, as we have noted, especially in the form of electricity, is very convenient for urban and large-scale industrial use. And centrally generated electricity can be transmitted over long distances. However, it is extremely expensive and inefficient to transmit it to dispersed centers with low demand, the kinds of communities in which most of the people of the developing world live. As a result, conventional rural electrification is only slowly reaching these areas. Even optimistic assumptions predict that not more than a quarter of developing countries' rural populations could have access to electricity by 1985.[48] Electricity is not a realistic near-term solution for the problem of cooking fuels—the major energy problem of developing countries—or for motive power for agriculture and transport.

No nation, in fact, can be said to be following either a wholly centralized or decentralized energy strategy. It is a matter of emphasis; most nations seek to maximize the use of whatever energy source they have. The problem is to decide which set of energy sources should be given priority.

3. Choice of Energy Source

Oil is the only known primary energy source that is both cost efficient and technically suitable for both centralized and decentralized energy. Unfortunately, oil is a depletable fuel and its long-term supply limits are becoming apparent. For modern industry and especially for transportation there is currently no substitute, though the search is on.

If used on a large scale globally, *coal* might prove to have hazardous effects on the ecosystems. It also requires large capital investments in infrastructure. However, it is a proven technology which, where resources exist, can be a valuable transition fuel to the post petroleum era. Known coal reserves are poorly distributed; only 17.4 percent of ultimately recoverable reserves are in the Third World and of these 82 percent are in China and India.[49] Coal may yet prove to be more plentiful in other Third World countries when they are more vigorously explored.

With careful planning and if a watchful eye is cast toward environmental and social impacts, *large scale hydropower* will undoubtedly play an increasing role in developing countries. With its physical potential only barely tapped, the major obstacle here is financing.

Nuclear energy currently faces a host of environmental, safety and security problems in the developed countries. In addition, the electrical grids of most developing countries are too small to meet the engineering requirements of even the smallest commercially marketed nuclear power plant.

Though it will be important to some countries, *geothermal energy* faces a number of technical, economic and environmental problems. In addition, commercially exploitable sites are not common except in a few developing countries. *Tidal power* doesn't appear likely to have much global application at this time.

Solar energy is ubiquitous and usable in four forms: photosynthesis, hydraulics, direct sunshine and wind. The problems with solar energy are not adequacy of primary energy but rather technological, economical and institutional constraints. Some technologies are proven; others are new. All need widespread testing and demonstration in developing countries—in both rural and urban areas—before we know whether they can compete economically and be accepted and maintained by local groups.

4. Improved Energy Economy

In the Northern industrialized countries, there is widespread agreement that economizing on the use of current energy offers the largest "new source" available in the short run. This is true for two reasons: excessive energy use exists because it is desired and because energy is often used inefficiently. Examples include leakage of warmed or cooled air from poorly insulated buildings, poorly tuned or inefficient cars, wasteful industrial processes and poorly planned urban complexes requiring undesirably long commuting. By reducing inefficiency, the North could make major savings with no sacrifice of personal enjoyment, comfort or luxury; and by making some sacrifices (e.g., carpooling and driving smaller cars), great savings could also be attained.

It has often been observed that conservation is not an important energy option in the developing countries. There are very few luxury automobiles and little space heating and cooling, except in the modern sector where it is essential for tourism.

In fact, although luxury use of energy in most developing countries is restricted to a small minority of the population, there is still great room for conservation through improved energy efficiency. Even the poorest (in some cases, especially the poorest) people use energy inefficiently. A.K.N. Reddy estimates that the use of simple mud stoves could double or triple the efficiency of fuel-wood use and hence cut the need for it to one-half or one-third of present levels.[50] Even slight improvements in indigenous, traditional stoves could have a large cumulative effect on preserving wood supplies.

Similarly, on the production side, planting fast-growing species of trees in village woodlots and urban fuel wood plantations (away from easy access by fuel-hungry residents) is an immediately feasible alternative. Charcoal, an increasingly preferred fuel, is made from wood by an old but inefficient method that retains no more than 25 percent of the energy content of the original wood. All the chargas and charoil are lost in this process as well. More modern techniques are available that produce perhaps 50 percent of the BTU value of the original wood, plus another 40 percent in captured chargas and charoil. Improved charcoal kilns, including portable varieties, are a simple and proven technology and would achieve considerable savings.[51] In cities, informal and "backyard" industries make bricks, beer, bread and do blacksmithing using wood or charcoal, very often by wasteful but inexpensive methods. The transportation fleets of many developing countries are old and poorly maintained, leading to inefficient use of gasoline.[52] Third World urban areas are often more poorly designed than Northern cities from the point of view of energy efficiency. In the modern commercial sector contemporary Western building designs are often employed. Many of these have been shown to be energy inefficient in the developed world. It is unlikely that they do any better in Third World cities. Even widespread, modern architectural adaptations, like the poor man's corrugated tin roof, are very poor insulators against heat and cold.

This incomplete listing of inefficiency in energy use is enough to suggest that the potential for saving is large--perhaps larger in the short run (up to five years) than any option on the supply side that will be available to developing countries.

Techniques and policies to improve the economy of this oil use will not only slow down foreign exchange outlays but increase the numbers of people who can use existing supply.

5. Choice of Transportation Strategy

Broadly stated, the issue here is one of "motive power," including transportation, but also plowing and tilling, and other moving needs. For the medium term, the most useful and efficient energy source to meet these needs will be oil.

However, new technologies are emerging that could one day ameliorate this dependence on oil; they include bioalcohols, more efficient batteries and hydrogen. Older means, such as coal-powered trains, may play a growing role in a few countries. Draft animal power is expanding in some parts of Africa where it previously did not exist and needs more encouragement where it is economically feasible. In urban areas, considerable oil savings can be achieved through a variety of means, including more widespread use of public transportation, pedal-powered vehicles, regular vehicle maintenance practices and re-designing cities to rationalize the relationship of residential areas and work places. The last is of particular importance. As in the industrialized countries, developing countries' urban areas have grown in an unplanned fashion. The difference is that their pace of growth is now much faster than that of the industrialized countries, and in many cases, this has led to further transportation bottlenecks and inefficiencies.

B. TECHNOLOGY AND RESOURCE PROSPECTS

1. Centralized Energy Technologies

a. OIL
Global and Developing Country Resources
For the foreseeable future, fossil fuels will play a vital role in the lives of the world's people. Of these fuels, petroleum is clearly the fuel of choice. It is relatively easy to extract, conveniently transported and used, and capable of being transformed into a variety of useful products from fuels to synthetic materials, fertilizer and medicines.

But oil's popularity is the source of the current concern with energy. The rise in the price of oil in this decade was, in part, an attempt to correct what, in effect, had been a worldwide subsidy of the use of energy. This subsidy was particularly damaging in the case of oil because it is a depletable fuel. The replacement price for oil—the cost of finding substitutes for it—has been and promises to continue to be higher than even the current price of oil.

The current geological consensus holds that the earth contains a little more than two trillion barrels of potentially recoverable petroleum, of which about 17 percent has already been consumed and another third is considered proved reserves. Hence, about half the world's oil is yet to be found.

A few geologists claim that even more oil than this will be discovered. How much will actually be exploitable (which is, after all, the pertinent question) will depend in part upon three factors: One is improved recovery from known and future oil fields (presently the global average recovery rate is only 25 percent but this may increase to 40 percent by the year 2000).[53] Another is new discoveries of oil. Finally, there is the ability to use known tar sands and oil shale deposits and to develop coal-based synfuels. All of these factors are strongly influenced by the price of oil.

The overwhelming share of known oil reserves is found in the developing world. However, all but a small proportion is in the OPEC nations. Excluding Mexico, the non-OPEC developing country oil producers account for only about 5 percent of the world's proved oil reserves.* In addition, the 70 oil-importing developing countries (OIDCs) possess less than 2 percent of the world's proven petroleum reserves.[54] Geological analysts generally agree that the distribution of ultimately recoverable oil reserves is roughly as follows:

TABLE 3

Middle East	30%—of which 1/10 has been consumed
Soviet Union	25%—of which 1/12 has been consumed
United States	10%—of which 1/2 has been consumed
Africa	10%—of which 1/20 has been consumed
Latin America[1]	8%—of which 1/5 has been consumed
Western Europe (including the North Sea)	3-4%—of which hardly any has yet been consumed
Other	13-14%

[1] *Note* that the Latin American proportion does not reflect the recent reserves additions of Mexico.

SOURCE:
U.S. Geological Survey's "Latin America's Petroleum Prospects in the Energy Crisis," U.S.G.S. Bulletin 1411, 1975, cited in D. Hayes, *Rays of Hope* (New York: W.W. Norton and Co., 1977), p. 36.

However, if the recent experience in Mexico holds any relevance for other areas in the developing world, these estimates may be revised upward considerably, with possible important policy considerations for alternative future energy strategies.

Tar sands and oil shales are not yet competitive in any area, though development is proceeding and some experts claim that Venezuela's heavy oil (from tar sands) may soon be commercially exploitable. The only sizable known deposits of tar sands in the Third World are in Latin America (Trinidad and Tobago, Colombia and Venezuela). Oil shale deposits are more widely distributed; but only in two countries, Brazil and Morocco, is any commercial production being planned.

At least in theory, the exploitation of oil shale and tar sands could en-

*Mexico's proved reserves were revised this year to 40 billion barrels of proved reserves, making its resources alone more than all other non-OPEC oil producers. Recent press reports indicate that Mexico's total proved and probable reserves may be as much as 327 billion barrels, which would be nearly twice as much as Saudi Arabia's.

hance global petroleum reserves by a huge amount. Formidable and costly technical problems stand in the way of widespread use of these resources. Oil from shale, for example, is currently projected to cost $22-$42 /bbl.[55]

Prospects for Oil in Developing Countries

Two difficult problems facing developing countries in petroleum matters are (1) attracting exploration ventures to determine the extent of their resources and to finance development of these resources, or (2) financing the cost of oil imports with their own resources.

Exploration. Except in a very few countries, the developing world has hardly been explored for oil. A number of promising areas exist in Southeast Asia, the Amazon Basin and the African interior. Even with conservative resource estimates, three-quarters of Latin America's potential, and more than 80 percent of Africa's and Asia's potential, remains to be discovered and developed. The experience with Mexico may prove to be unique, but it does illustrate the large degree of uncertainty on the actual state of oil resources in developing countries.

Most of these countries lack the expertise and experience that the developed countries and the multinational oil companies have gained in exploration. A great deal of high-risk capital is needed, but it is rarely available in countries with a long list of other development priorities and few indigenous capital-generating resources.

Despite the fact that prospective oil areas in non-OPEC developing countries comprise as much as 13 million square miles compared to 4 million for all OPEC, 3 million in the U.S. and 30 million throughout the world, little effort has been made to explore these areas.[56] Most exploratory drilling (which in and of itself was depressed during the period of lowest oil prices in the Sixties) has been done in the developed countries, especially the U.S., and in areas where long-established fields exist.

The lack of exploration activity by international oil companies is caused by a combination of political and economic factors. Politically, the multinational oil companies feared expropriation of their investments once oil had been discovered, or sudden changes by the host government in terms of their agreements. Economically, their market orientation has generally been more toward developing exportable quantities rather than developing smaller deposits that might be of greater interest to local governments. Export orientation also accounts for the generally lower exploration rate in landlocked countries. Whether the political or economic motivation is more important in explaining the lack of exploration is in some dispute. If recent experience is a guide, where the potential for large scale oil resources appears good, then interested oil companies will work to find a political accommodation with the host government. Where the export potential appears marginal or physical and political access is difficult, the companies appear to show much less interest in exploration.

The prospects of exploration are slowly improving. Exploratory well drilling by the large oil companies is increasing though still inadequate. Some of the more advanced oil producers like Mexico, Brazil and Argentina are doing more of their own exploration, including offshore prospecting and even exploration in other developing countries. Part of the problem is the great expense and high risk associated with "wildcatting." Neither the private nor the international banking sectors are yet willing to enter this area.[57] The recently announced World Bank energy program with its collaborative undertakings aiming at stimulating exploration may be of some help, particularly to areas of smaller potential. Another growing problem is the question of sovereignty over offshore oil fields, especially in the areas of traditional contention such as Southeast Asia.

Petroleum Development Costs

Once oil is found, attracting capital to finance its development is less of a problem. Still, the infrastructural costs of developing an oil industry are formidable. They include, for example, refineries, pipelines, distribution and marketing mechanisms. A relatively small number of oil producing countries have actually entered this area, though the trend is in this direction (except for very high technology areas such as off-shore oil development).

Rapid development of oil fields, particularly those off-shore, combined with routine and accidental ship discharges of oil, and natural seepage could seriously affect the biological productivity of marine areas. The recent tendency of the oil companies to build huge refinery complexes in some developing country areas, in part to escape environmental restrictions (e.g., the Caribbean and Southeast Asia), is of potential concern. Air pollution from internal combustion engines is already a worry in many developing country cities, as it is in the industrialized countries. Finally, fossil fuel combustion, in general, releases sizable amounts of carbon dioxide into the atmosphere. The long-term climatological effects of CO_2 buildup are as yet unknown but potentially very harmful.[58]

Oil Import Costs

The vast majority of developing countries import oil, and they are deeply concerned about the costs. Most of these nations are very oil dependent, and hence many of their economies were particularly hard hit by the recent oil price increases. The proportion of petroleum as a share of total imports, in one year, more than doubled in Tanzania, Cuba and India and tripled in Guinea.[59] Compounding the problem is the fact that higher oil prices boost the cost of other imports, such as food and manufactured goods, which are made with oil-intensive products or transported by oil-fueled vehicles.

With a total external debt of $175 billion (1978), the OIDCs are in a difficult position. For most of them, access to multilateral financial institutions like the World Bank and IMF is their principal means of acquiring financial assistance. Recent projections of non-OPEC developing countries' oil import demands for 1985 range as high as 5.2 MBD which would cost $45 billion a year (at June 1979 prices). Unless alternatives to oil are found, this near doubling of the OIDCs' oil bill could seriously damage development prospects.

b. NATURAL GAS

Most natural gas supplies are found with and, where possible, developed with petroleum deposits. In general, natural gas is not now a major part of the energy supply of any developing country. Even the OPEC countries with more than a third of the world's proven gas reserves accounted for only 9 percent of 1977 production. In fact, the non-OPEC developing countries have a somewhat higher rate of production in relation to reserves than OPEC (8 percent compared to 5 percent). Unfortunately, about a quarter of this production is flared for lack of a market.[60] Three kinds of uses could be (and are being) developed for natural gas: (a) exporting it by pipeline or in the form of liquid natural gas (LNG), (b) using it in the producing country for commercial and domestic purposes, and (c) reinjecting it (associated gas only) into oil wells.

Very little natural gas in now exported. The costs of pipelines and handling facilities are significantly higher than the prices of competing and available fuels. Until the advent of LNG, overseas transport was unfeasible. Now, the natural gas export market for developing countries is potentially much greater. However, serious cost and safety problems threaten to dampen the long-term prospects for LNG. The costs of pipelines and storage facilities at both ends of the journey and of cryogenic tankers are formidable. The U.S., a potentially major consumer of LNG, may not prove to be one if the government requires the LNG consumer to bear the full cost of the LNG rather than have it absorbed by cheaper domestic gas ("incremental pricing").[61] This may make it uneconomic compared with the costs of other non-conventional alternatives such as solar energy, or coal and waste gas.

Increasingly, developing countries are using their gas supplies domestically for thermoelectric generation, fertilizer and other petrochemical products and domestic fuels. The non-OPEC developing countries, in particular, have tended to use their gas domestically more than OPEC producers (63 percent of production in non-OPEC countries is commercially utilized, of which only a fifth is exported).[62]

One domestic option of recent interest is to reinject associated gas into oil wells as a form of secondary recovery, thus boosting oil production and conveniently storing gas that cannot now be easily used. Until recently, the necessary substantial investment in special equipment prevented this option from being exercised. But countries as diverse as Saudi Arabia and Chile are now undertaking it.

c. COAL

Despite the fact that global reserves of coal are at least ten times greater than known or anticipated petroleum and gas reserves, they play a minor role in all but a handful of developing countries. Only about 17 percent of ultimately recoverable reserves are thought to be located in these countries and currently they contribute only 6 percent to the world's coal production.

A major reason for this may be that most developing countries embarked on their modernization efforts after World War II when oil rapidly supplanted coal as the major commercial energy source. The most "coal-developed" countries have been developing a modern economy for a relatively long period. India, South Korea, China and Turkey in Asia and Mexico, Colombia and Brazil in Latin America are examples.

For the same reason, little exploration has been done in developing countries to ascertain the extent and quality of coal resources. The developing countries' very low share of coal resources may, in fact, be underestimated. In those countries where oil and gas have been found, coal resources have often been located as well—Iran, Indonesia, Nigeria and Mexico, to name a few.

The reasons for oil's ascendancy over coal point to some of the problems inhibiting coal's development even where resources have been identified. Coal development requires large capital investments for extraction and handling equipment, a large labor force to work the mines and transportation equipment including railroads to haul the coal economically. Its economic uses are more limited than oil's and usually require operation on a larger scale to be considered economic (though this may not be the case when small deposits are worked for a local market). These conditions and the capital to create them often are lacking (except for labor) in many developing countries, especially in the face of cheaper alternatives. The coal exploration and production part of the World Bank energy program may help to stimulate more investment in this area.

International trade in coal is very limited (5-6 percent of world production). What trade exists is mostly in coking coals for industrial smelting. [63] The major use of coal is in thermoelectric generation, although some countries continue to use it for rail transport, domestic heating and some synthetic material production.

Coal has an even greater negative ecological impact than oil. Extraction methods usually seriously deface the landscape, causing erosion, disturbance of aquifers and pollution of streams. The long-term health effects on miners and the dangers of explosions and mine collapses are major problems. And burning coal also releases large amounts of pollutants and carbon dioxide, as it does with oil.

A number of alternative ways of using coal have emerged over the years. One of the more recent ones is fluidized-bed combustion, which burns coal more efficiently and cleanly, and is available at different size scales of operation. Various coal conversion technologies are being developed, including coal gasification and liquefaction, as well as some intermediate solid-liquid states. The only country known to develop any of these commercially in recent years is South Africa with its coal-gasoline (which it has been producing since 1955). The coal conversion technologies are typically highly complex and inherently large-scale. Moreover, enormous capital investments would be required for such "synfuels" to be able to provide an effective alternative for current uses of oil, as the U.S. is beginning to perceive when it examines the implication of its crash 10-year proposed plan. Among developing countries, India is the only one known to have contemplated a coal liquefaction capacity, because of its well developed coal industry. Yet, even there it may prove uneconomic.

In general, coal is an economically feasible alternative where transportation, processing and marketing structures (including urban centers) are relatively more developed. Because of such infrastructure needs, the marginal cost per ton of coal is generally assumed to be cheaper in the North than in the South ($50 /ton of capacity vs. $75 /ton).[64]

d. NUCLEAR ENERGY

The commercial use of nuclear energy is less than a quarter century old. Technology is still in the development stage, and major problems remain unsolved including fear of weapons proliferation, radioactive waste, disposal of decommissioned power plants, rising capital costs and the costs and safety of operating nuclear power plants.

The attractions of nuclear energy include the absence of air pollution (barring the accidental venting of gases) and disturbance of terrain, its large concentration of power and the prestige value of advanced technology. Implicit in this last idea is the notion that a country with a nuclear energy program will earn greater respect from the developed world and at least move toward a capability of developing nuclear weapons.

Though the International Atomic Agency (IAEA) several years ago projected that nuclear energy could account for as much as 60 percent of electricity generation in developing countries by the year 2000, recent trends seem to indicate a far more problematic future for nuclear energy (currently the figure is 5 percent). A more recent IAEA estimate of the potential share that nuclear power could have of total installed electric capacity in developing market economies by the year 2000 was 27-40 percent, though even this seems rather optimistic. [65]

Nuclear Fuels

As with other energy technologies, one of the principal concerns is the adequacy of nuclear fuel. This problem is compounded by the safety of the fuels involved. The nuclear fuel cycle is complex and currently involves some shipment of spent fuels from reactor to reprocessing plant. This spent fuel contains an isotope of uranium and plutonium, the deadliest element known to man and a source of nuclear weapons material. Concern over the possible diversion of some of this plutonium for making weapons is one of the controversies surrounding the spread of nuclear power. The development of the "breeder" reactor is a method of using nuclear fuel that would vastly increase nuclear fuel supplies, but it would also lead to much greater production of plutonium. Hence, the need has arisen to develop stricter safeguards in the nuclear fuel cycle and greater international cooperation.

The question of disposal of nuclear wastes, some of which will remain dangerous for thousands of years, is only now receiving serious attention. Long term burial in stable geological formations is one solution, but such sites are few and would clearly require a great deal of international cooperation to transport and handle these wastes if nuclear energy is to be used worldwide. Other environmental problems exist, including the danger of a nuclear reactor core "meltdown" with the possible explosive release of radioactive steam, reactor decommissioning and the as yet undetermined effects of long-term low level radiation on human and animal populations.

The smallest commercially competitive reactors currently on the shelf are 600 MW in size.* With application of the electrical engineering rule that no one energy source should account for more than 10-15 percent of a grid system's load, this means a minimum grid size of 4000-6000 MW. [66] Only ten developing countries currently possess such a grid. The IAEA has been conducting research on smaller reactors (around 400 MW), and the Soviet Union is reportedly building a 440 MW reactor for Libya. But the trend is clearly toward a much higher minimum. [67]

Another economic problem complicating the spread of nuclear energy

---

*Recent trends even in developing countries are tending toward a higher competitive minimum, probably around 800-900 MW and higher, the "Candu" Canadian reactor being the only one marketed at 600 MW.

is the difficulty of evaluating its cost competitiveness. Because of its security applications, nuclear energy research and development is generally heavily subsidized by governments. This is also the case for nuclear fuel processing facilities and even insurance (in the U.S.). Precise costs of nuclear power plant construction are difficult to learn, but in the U.S. they are known to have risen dramatically in recent years.

Presently, five developing countries have commercial power reactors operating, and by 1980 another four are expected. By the year 2000, the IAEA estimates that nearly 30 developing countries could be producing nuclear energy commercially.[68]

Future expansion of nuclear power will depend in some measure upon political negotiations between the industrial countries and the developing countries. The decisions of the former countries on internal nuclear development will also influence the outcome, just as they have set the stage for the present controversy. At the heart of the matter is the question of whether nuclear supplier nations can control access to and development of nuclear energy technology and fuel supplies for other nations. The current U.S. position, which is strongly against nuclear power technologies capable of military diversion, has encouraged the establishment of guidelines by the Nuclear Supplier's Group to discourage sales of this kind and the convocation of the two-year-long International Nuclear Fuel Cycle Evaluation to find technical and institutional ways of making the fuel cycle relatively safer.

e. LARGE-SCALE HYDROPOWER

Present Use and Costs. The large-scale generation of electricity by falling water is probably the most widespread non-oil commercial energy source in the developing countries. About 44 percent of non-OPEC Third World electricity production comes from hydropower today. Potential capacity has barely been tapped. Currently, the developed countries with only 30 percent of the world's hydropower potential account for 80 percent of the world's production.[69] By 1980, hydropower could account for as much as 68 percent of non-OPEC Third World electric generation.[70]

Hydropower is attractive because it can generate large quantities of power from a clean and renewable indigenous energy source. And other uses can be made of a dam site, including irrigation, municipal water supplies, fisheries, recreation and flood control. This enables the project's costs to be spread smong other income-generating enterprises.

Hydropower is highly capital-intensive; operating costs are minimal by comparison. Construction costs are usually about $600/KW, although multipurpose projects may help recoup these costs. As with any electricity generation project, transmission and distribution costs are high; but in many hydropower projects they have been as much as half again the cost of construction. In large part this is true because hydropower is site-bound; and very often, the best hydropower sites are in remote mountain regions far from population centers.

Some countries find it difficult to integrate a hydropower project's electricity output into their grid. Outside of urban areas, local electric demand tends to be weak, and grid interconnections not very widespread in many developing countries. If electricity-intensive industries do not locate nearby, remote hydropower projects may be underutilized for long periods.

A number of other costs are associated with large-scale hydropower including biologically harmful variations in the downstream volume of water, the spreading of water-born diseases in slow-moving bodies of water like reservoirs and decreased flow of sediment (which is useful fertilizer in some areas). Reservoirs may displace valuable crops, timber land and even people in some instances. If watershed erosion controls are not instituted with the dam project, siltation may fill up the reservoir and decrease its potential electricity output.

Financing Needs and Sources. International lending institutions play a large role in many Third World hydropower projects because of the large initial capital investment required. A significant fraction of these costs require foreign exchange for construction equipment, technical assistance and power generation equipment.

Some of the more advanced developing countries, typically those with large hydropower programs, like Brazil and India, are assuming a greater role in financing and planning hydropower development. More prosperous developing countries have been able to attract a large share of private banking sector financing for hydropower projects.

In general, power development, of which hydropower is a major part, has been steadily rising as a share of total Third World borrowings. In 1974, it was 13 percent and is expected to rise to as much as 30 percent in the next decade.[71]

In summary, hydropower is expected to play a leading role in the Third World energy development.

f. OTHER CENTRALIZED ENERGY SOURCES

Geothermal Energy. Geothermal energy has been used for centuries for mechnical energy and water and space heating. Geothermal electrical generation is a technology of considerable promise for areas with suitable resources.

Geothermal energy uses the heat of volcanic activity near the surface of the earth and heat associated with hot springs and salt brines. Like hydropower, it is site-specific. Still, many developing countries have significant geothermal potential, and a number have started power generation, including Mexico, El Salvador and the Phillipines.

A given geothermal site is adaptable to any size development. Modular units are now available ranging from 400 KW to 4.5 MW with much higher sizes possible. Hence, geothermal energy may be as adaptable to rural areas as to urban. With the possible exception of hydropower projects (with consistently high load factors), dry steam geothermal energy has lower average costs than other centralized conventional technologies, depending upon the steam supply quality, market proximity and the difficulty of exploration and development.

Exploration is similar to that for oil and gas, and costs may range upward from $100,000 per well. On the other hand, the capital costs of the generating plant and operating costs are usually less than conventional alternatives and about competitive with hydropower.[72]

Average electricity production costs of geothermal generation range from 4-9.2 mils/KWh; and if exploration and transmission costs are included, costs range up to 13.8 mils/KWh, as compared to other conventional alternatives, which range in average costs from 6-27.6 mils/KWh.[73] The World Bank has financed two geothermal projects recently, and USAID has provided geothermal technical assistance for the Philippines and Indonesia. With World Bank funding, a 10 MW project for Kenya is now under constructon.

Major technical problems include the corrosive nature of minerals in wet steam and brines, resulting in the need for specialized alloys, steam separation and reinjection equipment. This last piece of equipment minimizes the environmental impacts of land subsidence and chemical pollution that might occur if wet steam and brine were not returned to the geothermal reservoir.

Tidal Energy. The extent of known potential for tidal energy is considerably less than that of geothermal energy. Given the costs involved, a large tidal variation is needed to generate sufficient power for tidal energy projects to be cost effective. The use of a variety of new techniques, high voltage transmission and pumped storage has smoothed out supply variations to meet regular and peak electricity demand. Still, tidal power is not yet cost competitive with any other conventional alternative.

A mean tidal range of 4-5 meters is a minimum tidal power requirement. There are only a few known places in developing countries that meet this requirement, the largest being the San Jose Gulf area of Argentina and the western coast of India.

2. Decentralized Energy Technologies

a. ELECTRICITY FROM THE SUN: SOLAR CELLS

Made of silicon and arranged in arrays up to as high as a few tens of kilowatts, photovoltaic cells (PVCs) are developing into a promising technology for local electricity generation.

Theoretically, the potential for electricity generated by the sun is vast. On a clear day near the equator, each square meter of the earth's surface receives about 6-8 KWh of solar radiation. Broadening the area to include the region between latitudes 40° N and 40° S, a conservative average would be solar insolation of about 4 KWh per square meter per day. In theory, if only 2 percent of this sunlight were converted with 20 percent efficiency, some 3.6 billion tons of coal equivalent energy could be produced—or nearly three times the present developing countries' total commercial energy consumption. However, efficiencies as high as 20 percent are still only obtained under laboratory conditions. Current applied technology doesn't range beyond 10 percent. There is great promise in direct sunshine if the technology to harness it becomes economically practical.

First developed in the U.S. in the mid-1950s, total cumulative production of solar cells was 2 MW by 1977. Their present employment has been in intermittent uses of small amounts of electricity, especially telecommunications. However, some experimental irrigation pumps in developing countries also use them as well and appear promising.

The price of solar cells has fallen dramatically with large recent purchases from the U.S. Department of Energy (DOE). From $300-$500/peak watt (Wpk) in the early 1970s, they have fallen, in some cases, to as low as $7-10/Wpk for flat arrays and $4-6/Wpk for concentrating arrays. DOE's goal is to attain prices of $0.50/watt by 1986 and $0.10-0.30/watt by 1990.[74] At these prices, widespread on-site use of solar cells would be economically feasible.

A number of problems remain before this can become a reality. Most of these problems are technical and economic, involving improvement in efficiency of the solar cells, storing the energy, protecting and prolonging the life of the solar cells, finding better and cheaper materials and ways of mass producing the cell.

b. HEAT FROM THE SUN: ENERGY FOR FARM, INDUSTRY AND HOME USE

Perhaps the cheapest, most immediate application of solar energy is through *low temperature technologies*. These are usually highly adapted to end-use and are easily constructed and maintained locally. *Solar cook-*

ers and ovens have been around for at least 20 years. While technically successful, past designs have failed to find cultural acceptance. A number of groups are currently working to overcome this problem, as well as to reduce costs. One practical problem is the fact that the inflexible household routine is to cook indoors or to cook in the evening and early morning hours when sunlight is not adequate. Thus far, the costs of gathering or buying wood have not been high enough to make adjustments in these routines acceptable.

Another basic need that solar technologies could meet is water heating. The basic technology is not new; and in parts of the southern U.S., solar water heaters were relatively common until World War II. Currently, 20 percent of Israel's households have solar water heaters. Hundreds of thousands are sold in Japan each year, and in Australia the figure is a million and a half.[75] Developing country use is limited, but some countries like Niger make and market their own. They are of particular use in developing countries for hospitals, rural clinics, schools, hotels and small restaurants and can be constructed on site.

Solar drying is probably the most widespread solar technology in the developing countries because of its simplicity. Crops such as chile peppers, coffee and tobacco have been solar dried for centuries—as has the family laundry. Improved enclosures can prevent wastage from insects, moisture and rodents and can raise the heating temperature to speed the process. Improved solar crop drying designs have potentially wide immediate application.

Space heating and cooling. Two basic modes exist to use solar energy for this purpose: passive designs and active ones. Passive solar heating and cooling have been employed by all cultures for centuries; and traditional designs are often fine-tuned to local construction, environment and social compatibility. Examples include thick stone or adobe house walls, thatched roofs, raising houses on stilts and the use of shade trees. Certainly in the industrialized countries but even in the rural and urban areas of many developing countries, these traditional designs have given way to less effective modern ones. Improved traditional designs, use of stronger materials and better site planning could enable these traditional designs to be used with great potential energy savings.

Active systems employ flat plate air or water heaters and a mechanical fan. Air heaters may use different kinds of storage devices, including rocks or chemicals. Active systems have the advantage of potential multi-use, heating or cooling space as well as the domestic water supply. Space heating with active systems has been technically and economically more feasible than cooling and is likely to spread faster in the cooler industrialized countries than in most developing countries. In addition, though technically simple, its sizable material costs will slow its growth in these countries.

Solar Distillation. This technology has been developed for decades. The principal technical problems include better structural design and dealing with corrosion and salt accumulation. Small solar stills may compare favorably with small fossil fuel-fired stills in terms of cost per thousand liters of water; they have the advantage of being highly modular and not dependent on complex machinery or imported fuel.

Other Solar Technologies. Most designs for *solar refrigeration* utilize absorption cooling cycles and have not been commercial successes. They are very expensive and require careful maintenance and monitoring. A project in the Philippines plans to use some solar refrigeration, but we know of none that is now operative in developing countries.[76]

A possible significant energy saver for business enterprises may be in the use of intermediate temperature technology. This is particularly applicable for solar process heat, especially as preheaters in combination with conventional fuels. Many food, textile and other industries require hot water, steam air and other fluids at temperatures up to 300°C, which can be supplied by solar water heaters at potentially significant conventional economic savings. The solar flat plate and the solar parabolic semi-cylindrical trough concentrating collectors are the principal technologies that can be used. The U.S. is testing a variety of such designs in industrial settings, though capital costs are such that they cannot yet compete with conventional alternatives.

Solar mechanical power using concentrating collectors dates as far back as 1913 with a 38 KW capacity irrigation pump experiment in Egypt. Solar thermal irrigation pump designs are now being demonstrated in a variety of developing countries though they are not yet cost competitive. Moreover, the large equipment and other materials cost and maintenance needs, limit the degree of future cost reductions. Until the price of competing energy sources rises significantly, they are likely to remain uncompetitive.

High temperature solar thermal systems are largely confined to thermoelectric generation, mostly with a steam medium. One experimental American design now generates steam for a 100 KW electric turbo generator.[77] Another U.S. Government effort is a "power tower" system capable of generating 5 MW which costs $21 million. It is hoped total system costs will eventually range from $1,000 to $2,000 per KWe.[78] Many technical and structural design and environmental problems exist with power towers; it will be well into the 1980s, at least, before these problems are resolved.

c. POWER FROM THE WIND

For over 2,000 years, man has captured the wind for mechanical and motive power. When the wind blows at roughly 9 meters per second, it provides the equivalent of half a kilowatt per square meter of windmill area (the area circumscribed by the fan blades). For the world as a whole, approximately 20 billion kilowatts theoretically may be available.[79] Generally speaking, equatorial areas have weak wind regimes, but generalized estimates are not very useful for determining site potential, since local topographical, seasonal and diurnal factors cause great variations in wind speed and duration.

The major areas for technical development include improving the efficiency of design and augmenting power. Low cost small applications using simply constructed, local materials would be especially useful for developing countries but need more research, development and actual testing in marketable areas.

Costs of wind machines vary with capacity and design. For wind-electric units they range from as little as $450 (.2KW) to $30,000 (for up to 5KW capacities).[80]

No comprehensive records exist of the operation of wind machines in developing countries, although many ventures have operated successfully for many years. But there have been frequent failures. Common reasons for these are lack of supervision and maintenance, lack of spare parts, improper siting or design selection and failure to enlist village interest in proprietorship of the wind machines.

d. ENERGY FROM PLANTS AND TREES

Wood fuels. Wood is by far the world's most important fuel, in terms of numbers of people dependent upon it. Yet until recently, this energy source has been almost totally neglected by scientists and most foresters (who have been concerned only with lumber—not fuelwood). No agreed estimates exist as to the extent of forest areas, the rate of depletion and replacement of forests, including how different species grow in harsh climatic conditions. Little is known of how efficiently fuelwood is used in cooking or rural industries, for example; nor has there been much study of the best ways to replenish wood supplies (e.g., plantations vs. village woodlots) or the social and economic relationships affected by changes in fuelwood use.

For many developing areas, the real energy crisis is a wood fuel problem that in some areas threatens to disrupt the social fabric of rural and urban areas. Rapid population increase and a desire for a better standard of living have combined to put pressure on forests for fuelwood supplies and crop and pasture lands. The result has been accelerated deforestation in many areas, erosion and increasingly scarce fuelwood supplies. Even greater deforestation exists around many urban centers where the concentration of demand is much greater and the use of charcoal more widespread.

Improvement in fuelwood cultivation and use is one of the few areas where action is likely to have immediate results. Because the technology of using fuelwood has remained unchanged for centuries in many places, improvement in cooking stove efficiencies, for example, could save the equivalent of millions of tons of wood. Afforestation and reforestation programs, preferably based on fast growing species suitable for easy use as fuel, are necessary, but have generally been either quite inadequate to meet demand or non-existent. Trees have multiple benefits, providing fuel, shade, windbreaks, erosion control and ecological niches for many other life forms. One of the critical problems in reforestation projects is to find incentives for villagers to cooperate in growing and caring for woodlots and plantations. In some cases, land tenure patterns act as a disincentive to such cooperation. In other instances, local governments have not been motivated to deal with the problem.

Crop residues. Although reasonably good data are available on crop production, residues are seldom measured. Estimates of residues can vary significantly even for a particular crop. Yet in many areas they have already great importance as auxiliary or seasonal fuels for cooking. However, they also have other "higher" uses as cattle fodder and compost for fertilizer.

Biogas. Biogasification—the anaerobic fermentation of human, animal and plant wastes to yield methane gas—is a relatively new technology. It has a number of benefits including the methane fuel itself and a by-product called slurry, rich in nitrogen and suitable for fertilizer.

The technology, while not very complex, does require a significant capital investment (for poor families), a minimum number of cattle, and careful monitoring of the biogasification process. Usually, biogas projects succeed where overnight corraling of domestic animals in one place is the custom. Otherwise dung collection becomes very difficult. For most rural areas of developing countries some multifamily scale of operation is likely to be the most economically viable, although where this has been tried formidable problems of organization and cooperation and questions of how to distribute the gas and fertilizer have been encountered.

Biomass technology is most advanced in Asia, particularly India, China and Taiwan, where the use of cow dung as a fuel is traditional. The Chinese (PRC) appear to have a large-scale program using biodigesters, particularly in the southwestern provinces where many have been installed in communes at the family level. But the Chinese effort is successful partly because of excellent organization and the selective exploitation of certain traditional values and practices.

Prospects for biogas technology are based primarily on the availability of and willingness to use waste to produce fuel, on climate (in colder areas), and particularly on willingness to cooperate in supplying and caring for the biodigestion process and in the distribution of the gas and slurry fertilizer.

Pyrolysis. This energy technology consists of the selective destruction of cellulitic material in an enclosed environment with high heat and little air. Charcoal from wood is probably the most common product, but combustible oil and gas are also attainable. Modern designs can produce combustible products from all kinds of organic materials and hence widen the utilizable resource base.

Charcoal, though costlier than wood, is highly sought after in both rural and urban areas because it burns cleaner, is less bulky and has more heat energy per unit of mass. Moreover, its heat output is more uniform, which makes it prized for cooking and especially for small scale industry.

A variety of commercial kilns now exist, and other more efficient ones are being developed. Some of the more advanced varieties, such as pyrolytic converters, are generally expensive, technically complex and most useful on a village scale basis at the minimum. Simple improved kilns, including portable varieties and large ones using more efficient variations on traditional techniques, hold more promise.

Bio-Alcohol Fuels. The technology for using ethanol and methanol mixed with conventional fuels or by themselves dates back at least to World War II. Brazil has set up a large-scale program of mixed alcohol and gasoline fuels, and the U.S. Department of Energy has a similar national goal for 1987.[81]

The advantages of using alcohol with gasoline are that it is renewable, it has a high octane rating and hence power, it is more efficient for engine operation and it is less polluting than straight gasoline. Technical problems that appear resolvable include vapor lock, faster burning and the need for carburetor adjustments. More significant technical-economic problems are the large scale of distilleries needed, the cost of preparing the feed stock for distilling and the use of available land for growing fuel rather than food.

For many developing countries bioalcohol fuels could be a possible substitute for kerosene. The present widespread use of kerosene in rural and urban areas for cooking and heating (and its soaring price) warrant greater attention to applied research into the possibility of bioalcohol substitution.

e. SMALL-SCALE HYDROPOWER

Once a very widespread source of mechanical power and even electricity (in the U.S.), small-scale water technology is only now being reevaluated favorably. It offers the advantages of being renewable, clean, environmentally benign relative to larger-scale projects and suitable for small, local loads.

The potential for small-scale hydropower is unknown because hydrological studies, aside from being incomplete for most developing countries, have ignored the power potential of small streams. It can safely be assumed to be rather large. Moreover, much of it may be near population centers. One international solar energy workshop in Tanzania, a rather dry country, found that a substantial number of the rural population lived adjacent to year-round streams large enough for small-scale hydropower development. Another workshop noted that in energy-starved Nepal, enough steam power potential exists to provide 3.5 KW per person. By comparison, the U.S.'s current installed hydropower and thermal capacity equals 2.4 KW per person. [82] Up to a third of China's (PRC) total developed hydropower capacity is thought to be from small-scale hydropower. [83]

Chinese mini hydro units vary from as low as ½ KW to 28 KW. Prices for some U.S. units with power conditioning accessories range from $330-1300/KW (in units from 3 KW up to 18 KW). [84]

f. DRAFT ANIMALS

There are 1.4 billion draft animals in the developing world—about one draft animal for every two persons. Their work effort potential is equal to about .1-.3 quadrillion BTUs (Quads). [85] By comparison the U.S. in 1975 used 72 Quads. But their global distribution is quite skewed, ranging from as high as 1:2 to 1:4 (draft animals to man) in India to none at all in tsetse fly-ridden parts of Africa. It is generally assumed that a draft animal's use is about 75 percent farm work and 25 percent transport and domestic use. [86]

Major problems with current uses of draft animals include lack of feed and ill health, which reduce efficiency to a fraction of its potential.

Draft animal use appears to be slowly declining in many areas for a variety of reasons; but in those areas where cultivation is still by hand and the man to land ratio favorable, they could be a valuable aid, aside from their uses as meat, milk, hides and dung for fertilizer and fuel.

For cultures not used to using draft animals, they are not a simple technology. They require careful husbandry practices in feeding and health care. An industry capable of providing harness and equipment must also be developed. Finally, they need either crop residues or the equivalent of at least one-third of an acre per animal for grazing.

g. SMALL-SCALE RENEWABLE ENERGY POTENTIAL

Unfortunately, opinion among analysts is tending to polarize on the merits of small-scale renewable energy (SRE). Experts on these energy sources often become advocates or even evangelists, as do experts on conventional large-scale energy. Small-scale renewable devotees are indignant at the risks being proposed by nuclear advocates, and the latter are shocked at the suggestions that solar technology be adopted by policy makers in its present untried state. And so each side extols the virtues of its own solutions and assails the other. There is little spirit of honest inquiry.

The truth is that we do not know how well SRE will perform in Third World villages, market towns and urban slums. Nobody has ever tested the technologies and recorded and made public the results. Many micro-hydroelectric facilities have been installed in China and a few elsewhere, but there is no detailed reporting on cost, performance, local acceptability and maintenance, operating and repair problems. Millions of biodigesters are reported in China and thousands in India but again without adequate public reporting on results. A few windmills have been erected in Africa but nearly all have failed when left to the care of African villagers. Solar thermal and photovoltaic pumps are being tried in a few Third World villages but as yet no results are in. Solar cookers have been tried for two decades in a handful of Third World villages with discouraging reports of the unwillingness of the villagers to use them. Community tree plots and national reforestation programs have been attempted and have tended to prove that new tree species hold considerable promise, but that administrative, land tenure and political problems are formidable. In general, the story on SRE is that the jury is still out. One of the most important tasks is to set in motion thousands of site tests of the more promising small-scale renewable energy systems.

Such tests are not without costs. Are these devices sufficiently practical and feasible to warrant such costs? Clearly they have some *a priori* advantages: First, they depend on wind, sun, flowing water and organic wastes—all primary sources that are inherently decentralized. Not all villages have all four such sources, but most tropical villages have some in sufficient amounts.

Decentralization may prove to be an enormously important advantage for rural areas and market towns. Thus far, centralized energy has made only very slow progress into the countryside. Grids of petroleum distribution have begun to spread, but only slowly; and unfortunately they will run into increasing trouble as oil prices rise. Electrical grids have been very slow to reach beyond urban and suburban areas and even when they do, few can afford the hook-up charges and utility rates. When they do reach rural areas, their product—electricity—cannot economically help with cooking, the most important village energy need, or with draft power needs.

Second, the absolute magnitude of such energy sources in the Third World is great. Sunshine and organic mass are generally greater in tropical than temperate zones. Third, such technologies tend to be either positively beneficial to the environment—e.g., afforestation, solar cookers (by saving trees) and biodigesters (by returning animal and vegetable wastes to the soil)—or at least tend to have relatively little adverse impact on air, soil and water compared with large-scale technologies. Fourth, the cost trend for at least one device (i.e., solar cells) is expected to be downward as demand makes mass production possible. While these advantages do not prove that SRE devices are practical, they do offer sufficient promise to warrant widespread tests. If such tests are pressed vigorously and if the results are pooled and publicized, energy policymakers may be able to make decisions solidly grounded on the facts within a few years.

Meanwhile, until the facts are available, Northerners should be diffident about pushing SRE as a panacea for the South. It is not only unjustified by the present state of knowledge of the facts, but to the South it must sound suspiciously as if the North is saying, "You take the sun, wind, and wastes and we will take the oil, coal and nuclear power."

PART III: OPPORTUNITIES FOR SOUTH-NORTH COOPERATION IN ENERGY

A. INTRODUCTION

International consultation and cooperation on energy currently is handled piecemeal and incompletely in several forums and on a variety of topics. The Northern industrialized countries consult regularly on managing the adjustment to higher oil prices, emergency planning for oil supply interruptions, conservation and R&D. OECD and OPEC are in a dialogue about avoiding oil supply interruptions and on future oil prices. The nuclear suppliers club confers on avoiding weapons proliferation. And, the North, in cooperation with OPEC surplus foreign exchange nations, has worked out mechanisms for recycling these surpluses and helping low income importers to meet their bills

It is not certain that oil importing developing countries (OIDCs) would have an interest in participating in every one of these (and other related) forums, especially with the competing demands on the time of their qualified people. But at the same time it may be important for some of the international energy topics to be discussed in a South-North forum.

Here, we will discuss several topics for international cooperation to which a South-North Energy Dialogue might wish to devote some attention, beginning with a series of issues related to oil.

B. CANDIDATE TOPICS FOR SOUTH-NORTH DIALOGUE

1. Financing the Oil Import Gap and Beyond

Within weeks after the oil price rises of 1973, the IMF swung into action with proposals to help its members finance their oil and other import needs. An oil facility was established in August, 1974, followed soon by a 1975 oil facility. By May 1976, SDR 6.9 billion had been drawn. [87]* In addition, drawings from members' credit tranches and from the compensatory facility expanded greatly, with the year ending April 30, 1976, achieving a record high of SDR 7.0 billion in total drawings. The "Witteveen Facility" of $10 billion proposed in the Spring of 1977 has funds available to all members. It will come into effect when SDR 7.75 billion have been made available to the Fund.

OPEC nations have made major financial transfers to developing countries. These disbursements (net) amounted to $7.29 billion in 1977, not including unreported special oil pricing or oil credit arrangements between oil exporters and oil importing developing countries. [88] The OECD countries also increased financial flows to nearly $14.8 billion in 1977, compared with $11.3 billion in 1974. But these numbers were not large in comparison with the total deficit of the non-oil developing countries, which in 1976 came to $77 billion. [89]

There have been many proposals to expand funds available to help pay for oil and other imports. Some are aimed at only a modest expansion in existing facilities. Others plan to recycle a major part of the surplus funds in the hands of some oil exporters, plus Germany and Japan, so that Third World demand for Northern products will help to reestablish the health of the world economy. Among the more modest proposals are an expansion of the Witteveen Facility from $10 to $15 billion and the provision of an interest subsidy for low income countries financed by a special tax on oil traded in world markets. Expansion in IDA financing and a multilateral "co-financing" guarantee facility, under which OECD and OPEC countries would guarantee loans to developing countries, have also been suggested. [90]

Identified below are four of the more ambitious proposals for new international mechanisms to recycle massive funds from the surplus countries to those in the Third World that are in need of foreign exchange:

a. Senator Jacob Javits of the United States has proposed a $25 billion Growth Development Fund for a five-year period to be used to finance investment in developing countries in agriculture, industry and trade

---

*In the range of 8.5-9 billion U.S. dollars.

with priority to energy investments. The Fund would be financed by contributions from OECD and OPEC countries.

  b. The Government of Mexico proposed a long term recycling facility of $15 billion without a time limitation to help developing countries finance capital goods purchased from OECD countries. The facility would be financed by both private and public investments in surplus countries and would be administered by the World Bank.

  c. The Government of Venezuela suggested a joint OPEC/OECD Global Stimulation Plan funded by surplus OPEC and OECD funds amounting to some $20 to $40 billion over a 5 to 10 year period. It would be used to help non-oil developing countries increase their imports from industrial countries.

  d. An Investment Plan was prepared by the OECD staff for $5 to $10 billion of additional capital flows per annum for major increases in investments in developing countries to stimulate world economic activity. A major goal would be to encourage structural changes, including strengthening Third World production of food, energy, commodities and related infrastructure. It would be financed by equity and debt from private and commercial sources in OECD and OPEC.

  Two common threads run throughout these four proposals: First, an important purpose of each is to strengthen the world economy by stimulating Third World demand for OECD goods and services; and, second, each would be administered by existing International Financial Institutions (or in Javits' proposal a new institution is offered as an alternative).

  Although these massive capital transfer proposals are not exclusively directed at energy development, they do tend to find their origins at least partly in the problems of adjustment to the impact of the oil price rises and of recycling surplus funds that are largely accumulating in the hands of oil exporters. Since such transfer schemes are clearly energy related, the South-North Energy Dialogue may wish to address this subject.

2. Keeping Trade and Investment Channels Open

  By far the largest producer of foreign exchange to the South is trade. Rapid expansion of exports has taken place in the South, stimulating growth at home, particularly in the modern sector, as well as demand for imports of goods and services that are essential in development. Private investment plays a smaller role in the transfer of foreign exchange but is important in a number of fields for certain countries because it provides entrepreneurial and technological inputs and a conduit to Northern markets for Southern exports.

  But as certain nations of the South make gains in exports to the North, workers in the less competitive industries in the North are displaced and political pressures increase to limit trade and investment with the exporting South. Northern export industries that favor trade with the South and would be hurt if such barriers were erected have difficulty matching the pressures generated by the less competitive Northern industries and some labor unions. A Northern program of financial and other aid to help its own displaced workers—and union officials—to make the move to more competitive industries might do as much to help the economic health of the South (and of the world) as a comparable effort spent transferring public aid funds to the South. The South-North Energy Dialogue might wish to take note of this topic.

3. Expanding Production of Oil, Gas and Coal in the OIDCs

Many oil experts expect that the world will find about as much oil in the future as has been found to date and that about half of this oil will be found in oil importing developing countries (OIDCs). The exploration rate in these countries is low compared with exploration in other areas of equal promise. For example, the number of wells drilled per square mile in non-OPEC developing countries is only one for every 100 drilled in the United States on terrain of equal geological promise.[91]

What holds up the rate of exploration in the OIDCs? The answer is far from clear. In October 1976, the President of Shell Oil Company made a speech in which he blamed a poor investment climate in the OIDCs for the lack of exploration and called for an international program to guarantee investors against loss by reasons of expropriation.[92] On the other hand, Exxon is not persuaded that political risk is a very significant factor. In an unpublished but widely circulated paper dated June 1978, Exxon said that oil companies are willing to assume a potential political risk "apparently in direct relation" to the oil producing potential of the area. Political risk is hardly ever seen as an insurmountable factor, although temporary problems such as offshore boundary disputes, civil unrest and the like will clearly prevent exploration activity.[93]

The Trilateral Commission believes that political risks are important and has proposed that donors help OIDCs find and develop their indigenous energy sources including an expansion of the World Bank's initial efforts along these lines. The Trilateral Commission also proposed an International Center for Research and Exploration, which among other things would subsidize oil, gas, coal and uranium exploration projects. This is an important topic to the OIDCs, the multinational oil companies and the oil thirsty world. Perhaps a special study group to examine this topic should be sponsored by the South-North Energy Dialogue. To be unbiased, such a group should hear the views of both underexplored Third Eorld countries and oil exploration companies.

With respect to coal, present knowledge suggests that not many OIDCs have coal resources. However, present knowledge is not very great and some experts believe that much more coal will be found when it is looked for in earnest. If the Dialogue study effort is launched with respect to oil and gas exploration, consideration may well be given to encouraging exploration for coal in OIDCs also.

4. Oil Supply Security

The OECD countries have banded together to protect themselves in the event of an interruption in the supply of oil. Members of the OECD's International Energy Agency have agreed to an emergency allocation program under which they pledge to restrain consumption, build oil stocks, and to share oil resources, including emergency stocks, in the event of serious supply shortfalls. It is an open question whether OIDCs feel that the threat of oil supply interruption is great enough to warrant the significant investment of time necessary either to establish their own emergency plans or to negotiate arrangements to be covered under the plan of the IEA.

5. Oil and Other Energy Conservation

The chief measure emphasized by the IEA in its efforts to defend against oil supply interruptions was to cut demand. These efforts have included declarations, searching reviews with published finger-pointing exercises and pledges of best efforts to do better. The biggest oil consumer has, in fact, done little in the way of actual conservation.

As we noted above, there is little extravagant or conspicuous consumption of energy in the OIDCs, but there is a great deal of inefficiency. The remedy for inefficiency is capital investment in better energy, using technology and investment in training and planning to use better the existing amounts of energy rather than individual self-restraint. It is doubtful whether a finger-pointing exercise such as is conducted by IEA would be helpful to the OIDCs.

The aid-donor countries can help the South conserve energy in two basic ways. First, they can help to assess the problem and identify opportunities for improved energy use. There are many Southern scholars who could survey and quantify alternatives for each interested country to improve its energy economy, and point out specific opportunities. The aid-donor counries could help to finance such scholarly and analytical work. Second, the aid-donor countries can help finance energy efficiency programs undertaken by the OIDCs. If the latter undertake to conserve fire wood by marketing improved cheap stoves, this could be a worthy aid project. Similarly, aid projects could help to replace inefficient production machinery in industry, transportation or agriculture. Another target for such projects might be to improve inefficient production processes. These are only a few of the examples of opportunities for cooperation in conservation. The decision to take steps toward serious energy economy improvements and, if so, how to do it would, of course, be up to each developing country.

The Dialogue might include either the subject of energy use improvement in the North and OPEC or the subject of South-North cooperation to improve efficiency in the OIDCs, or both.

6. A Global Energy Balance Sheet

The first prerequisite for a sound plan for tomorrow is a good grasp of the situation today. In the field of developing country energy, the lack of facts about current energy regimes is a major problem. Little is known about energy use, current sources, potential supply and the gap of unmet needs in rural areas of the Third World. Little is known about the availability of primary renewable energy in these areas. Not much information is at hand about the physical performances of various machines to capture and make useful such energy in actual village situations nor about their costs, acceptability to local cultures, nor the best means of introducing them into villages. The same lack of information limits our understanding of medium-sized energy technologies that might supply energy to groups of villages. Finally, little is known about the impact of modern energy upon the economic and social life of Third World villages and urban slums. The most basic need is for one or more international organizations to gather the facts on current global energy supply, potential supply, demand and needs, and to analyze that information. Based on those analyses, these organizations could then more properly advise the international community of nations on the problems ahead for our planet and to stimulate debate and discussion of various scenarios for attacking those problems.

In the field of food and agriculture, international machinery exists to gather, analyze and disseminate such facts. The U.N. Food and Agricultural Organization, the World Food Council, the International Fund for Agricultural Development, and the Consultative Group on International Agricultural Research plus a series of specialized international networks could encourage and coordinate research. Energy has no counterpart for any of these organizations. The closest thing is the International Energy Agency, a unit of the OECD.

The Overseas Development Council a few years ago proposed the creation of a organization that could act as the keeper of a "global energy balance sheet."[94] The Trilateral Commission with a similar monitoring idea has suggested a fortified IEA as the institution to carry out such a mission. The ODC recommended it be done by a permanent staff of a newly established global political body (see Item 7 below) for which the title "World Energy Council" was suggested. [95]

The South-North Energy Dialogue might wish to consider the pros and cons of alternative international organizational arrangements to perform these functions. For example, should such organization(s) be technical or should it (they) be policy oriented? How can the many interested nations be fairly represented without reducing professional effectiveness? Should there be one organization to keep the global energy balance sheet and another to undertake analyses? Should these analyses be prescriptive or only diagnostic? Should the organization(s) deal only in global topics or should advice also be given to individual countries? These and other questions might very well be examined as a special project of the South-North Energy Dialogue.

7. Continuing the South-North Dialogue

The Trilateral Commission called attention to the need for a forum to advance the South-North dialogue that was discontinued after the end of CIEC. It recommended a small but representative "standing 'council' of top officials" from both South and North to "engage in a political and economic dialogue on global issues," a formulation very consistent with the "World Energy Council" proposed by the ODC. [96]

In the latter proposal, the staff of the "Council" would be permanent and would prepare the global energy projects. This is a topic the Dialogue may wish to consider.

8. Energy and the Environment

The Trilateral Commission has called attention to the fact that environmental concerns have delayed the development of energy supplies and recommends the creation of an independent committee of distinguished scientists (including some from the South) to consider the issue, possibly under OECD auspices. [97] The domestic environmental concerns of the South are similar in some respects and different in others from those in the North. Clearly, there are not yet in the South aroused citizen groups who oppose refineries, reprocessing plants, strip coal mining, etc. The more immediate environmental concerns of the South tend to be deforestation and erosion rather than industrial and water pollution. But there are also some internationally shared concerns, such as pollution of the oceans and safe disposal of nuclear wastes. There is also a shared concern about the growing (and still generally welcomed) practice by the North of exporting to the South its polluting industries. Another issue is the insistence on the part of some Northern donors (e.g., the U.S.) that certain environmental standards be met in the South as a condition of aid. Because of all these shared concerns, the Dialogue may wish to consider the subject of energy and the environment.

9. Managing Nuclear Energy

Guidelines for access to nuclear energy have been laid down by the Nuclear Suppliers Group made up of 15 Northern nations.[98] The United States as the chief nuclear supplier has imposed some additional rules of its own. The IAEA polices internationally agreed upon safeguards against weapons proliferation and also monitors the non-Proliferation Treaty. Proposals have been made for a "fuel bank" under international control to serve as a supplier of enriched fuel and institutions to reprocess fuel and dispose of nuclear wastes. Many proposals have been made to strengthen IAEA's inspection system as well.

Of wider significance are the current discussions of the International Nuclear Fuel Cycle Evaluation (INFCE). Composed of both suppliers and consumers, developed and developing nations alike, the 40 participants are grappling with the critical technical and institutional problems of improving the nuclear fuel cycle to make it safe against weapons proliferation. The underlying theme of the discussions is whether the world can have widespread use of nuclear energy without widespread nuclear weapons proliferation. The critical "back end" of the cycle where the problems of waste disposal and/or reprocessing arise is one of the major issue areas of these discussions and the focus for ongoing nuclear policy cooperation.

However, the crux of the problem remains political agreement, which the INFCE is not equipped to address. One alternative proposed by the Trilateral Commission is to establish a parallel effort "to explore the political and institutional arrangements needed to prevent proliferation," involving key Trilateral countries.[99] Finally, there is the question of minimum size of fission, breeder and eventually fusion units. The smallest nuclear fission power generating unit now commercially available is 600 MW. This would be suitable only for integrated electrical grids of 4000 to 6000 MW, because of the engineering reliability rule that a grid should not rely on any one power source for more than 10 to 15 percent of its supply. As breeders and perhaps eventually fusion generators come into commercial use, minimum sizes will escalate rapidly perhaps bypassing most developing countries because of size. At present, there is no forum that includes representatives of the developing countries to debate these issues. This may be a topic of particular interest to the Dialogue.

10. Development of Renewable Energy

a. Research and Development
There is a consensus that eventually the world will have to rely on the current income of energy from the sun, supplemented only by "lunar energy" in the form of tides and continuing thermal radiation from the earth's core that supplies geothermal energy.[100] Despite future dependence upon solar energy, it has not until recently fared well in the Research and Development budgets of the world. Attention to the subject is now increasing; in 1977 (the latest data available from OECD) it still was the smallest item in OECD budgets for R&D amounting to only 6.2 percent of those budgets. Within this amount, the bulk was reported to have been devoted to large-scale centralized units, which probably will not have immediate application for developing country energy needs. About three-quarters of the world's R&D in this field is supplied by one country—the United States. Solar R&D in the developing countries increases each year but is still small. A few countries have large-scale efforts, e.g., Brazil in bioalcohol fuels, India and Taiwan in biogas, and China in small-scale water power and biogas.

b. Site Testing
A number of small-scale renewable energy devices have been proven in laboratories and some (e.g., windmills and small hydrogenerators) have been proven in commercial use in Northern industrialized countries. There are also reports of widespread use of small hydroelectric generators and biodigesters in China and limited use of the latter in India. But with respect to the villages and urban slums of Africa, Asia (with the exceptions noted above) and Latin America, there is little knowledge of the practical utility of small-scale renewable energy. Site tests in perhaps 100 or more villages in sub-Saharan Africa are being planned by the USAID program and other donors are developing similar plans as well. Such tests will try to assess the physical performance of the more promising devices under village and urban slum conditions, costs, ownership and maintenance problems, cultural or sociological problems with the new technology, and the impact on village life of modern energy. A proposal is being considered by industrialized countries for coordinating such site tests as a result of an agreement reached during the July 1978 Summit meeting in Bonn.

c. Organizing Outside Support for R&D
A great many small research efforts on SRE are under way in universities and laboratories throughout the world. The very incomplete files of the Overseas Development Council contain information on 380 such ef-

efforts outside the United States, 175 of them in 50 developing countries. These researchers often express their need to be tied into a system that keeps them up to date on similar work elsewhere in the World. Many proposals have been made to provide such outside support. Henry Kissinger, when he was the U.S. Secretary of State, proposed an International Energy Institute;[101] the Trilateral Commission has suggested an International Center for Energy Research and Exploration, lumping R&D on SRE together with fossil fuel exploration.[102] The Overseas Development Council has suggested global R&D networks organized by topic similar to the networks of researchers on corn, wheat, rice, etc.[103] The ODC has also suggested a series of workshops of researchers to learn what kind of international support they believe would be most helpful to them.[104]

d. An International Solar Energy Development Fund

The Overseas Development Council has proposed establishment of an International Solar Energy Development Fund.[105] This Fund might be financed either through governmental contributions from OECD and OPEC countries as with the International Fund for Agricultural Development (IFAD); through a mix of governmental and private contributions as with the Consultative Group on International Agricultural Research (CGIAR); or through a modest (e.g., one cent per barrel) international tax levied on every barrel of oil traded internationally. This would amount to about $100 million per year.

The Solar Energy Development Fund (SEDF) might be administered by an IFAD equivalent or by a special consultative group chaired and staffed as is the CGIAR by either the World Bank or IFAD with functions such as the following:

i. Building solar energy institutions in developing countries. This would include costs of training personnel, equipment, laboratory buildings, and foreign experts. In a number of countries solar energy research institutes already exist and could be further strengthened. In other cases, such entities would need to be established. They would not normally engage in basic research but instead would (a) study what modifications are needed to adapt existing technology to local needs and conditions, (b) train a core of people in using such equipment and (c) monitor a series of field tests of such equipment (see #iii below).

ii. Finance national energy surveys in scores of developing countries to help them determine what general energy strategy (i.e., centralized or decentralized) and energy sources to pursue.

iii. Finance and help to design field tests of small solar equipment at the village level. The SEDF should seek to swell the current trickle of tests from hundreds into thousands.

iv. In some instances, SEDF may want to finance large-scale solar equipment to test its usefulness to the national grid.

v. Finance the dissemination of the more successful decentralized solar energy equipment to points of use throughout developing countries.

As the results of the tests mentioned above become available, a number of countries will want to make the more promising technologies available on a wide scale to villages or market towns throughout their country. SEDF might help to arrange financing for such technology extension including the use of its own funds. The $100 million per year suggested above may have accumulated by that time to a fund large enough to be significant even in the face of demand for funds for widespread application of solar technology. But in any event, the SEDF's focus should be to act as a financial catalyst to bring in larger amounts of funding in untried areas.

Concerning each of the subjects discussed above (R & D, Site Testing, and arrangements for international support and a special fund), the Dialogue may wish to consider including them in its activities.

11. Collecting Information on Traditional Energy

There is a tremendous need for more information on the amounts of traditional energy now used, the growth rates of supply and demand for these fuels and the obstacles to improving the traditional energy situation. Many recent Northern analyses of the global "energy" situation have been done, describing how much there is and when the world will run short. "Energy" in these analyses is defined to include only energy that is bought and sold in markets which are included in a system of national accounts. Thus, for the most part "energy" is limited to conventional energy, i.e. coal, oil, gas and electricity. It generally omits wood, charcoal, animal and crop wastes, and animal and human muscle power even though about 60 percent of the people in the world and 80 percent in the Third World depend almost exclusively on these traditional energy sources. The reason for this omission is understandable viz. no very reliable information exists with respect to traditional energy; nor even a good idea of the proper methodologies for gathering this information or what subject areas to include. The result is that virtually all of the world's attention is limited to conventional energy even though, as we noted in Part I of this paper, the crisis of traditional energy is more painful and far reaching than the crisis of conventional energy. It is a crisis of today rather than a potential crisis of the 1990s. The Dialogue may wish to consider the topic.

12. The Proposed UN Conference on Alternative Energy

A proposal has been approved by the UN General Assembly for a UN Conference on New and Renewable Sources of Energy to be held in 1981.

This would coincide with the 20th anniversary of the 1961 UN conference on "New Sources of Energy," the proceedings of which have served over the years as a landmark reference work to scholars interested in the subject. The South-North Energy Dialogue may wish to consider whether to support the Conference and, if so, what contributions to make.

FOOTNOTES

1. Marion J. Levy, Jr., *Modernization and the Structure of Societies—A Setting for International Affairs,* Vol. 1 (Princeton, N.J.: Princeton University Press, 1966), pp. 10-12, 35.

2. Harrison Brown, *The Human Future Revisited: The World Predicament and Possible Solutions* (New York: W.W. Norton and Company, Inc., 1978), p. 21.

3. Historically, those countries reaching a PQLI of 77 or more have been those that are meeting the basic human needs of their people and a decent quality of life. See Morris David Morris, *Measuring the Condition of the World's Poor—The Physical Quality of Life Index* (New York: Pergamon Press, 1979).

4. United Nations, *World Energy Supplies 1950-74* and *1971-5,* Doc. nos. ST/ESA/STAT/SER, J/19 and ST/ESA/STAT/SER. J/20 (New York: 1975).

5. T.L. Sankar, "Alternative Development Strategies with a Low Energy Profile for a Low GNP/Capita Energy-Poor Country: The Case of India," in *The Energy Syndrome,* ed. by Leon N. Lindberg (Lexington, Mass.: D.C. Heath and Company, 1977).

6. Derek E. Earl, *Forest Energy and Economic Development* (Oxford: Clarendon Press, 1975).

7. George Beier, *et. al, The Task Ahead for the Cities of the Developing Countries,* World Bank Staff Working Paper No. 209 (Washington, D.C.: World Bank, July 1975), p. ii.

8. Edward Jaycox, "La Banque Mondiale et la Pauvreté dans les Villes," *Finances et Developpement,* Volume 15, Numero 3, Septembre 1978, p. 10.

9. Lester Brown, *In the Human Interest, A Strategy to Stabilize World Population* (New York: W.W. Norton & Co., 1974), pp. 108-109.

10. UN, *World Energy Supplies, 1950-74.*

11. Beier, *The Task Ahead.*

12. "Yes, Small Can Be Beautiful," *The Economist,* Vol. 267, No. 7028, 13 May 1978, p. 112.

13. Robert d'A. Shaw and Donald R. Sherk, "The International Utilization of Labor and the Multinational Corporation in the Pacific Basin," in *Pacific Basin Development: The American Interests,* ed. by Harald B. Malmgren (Lexington, Mass.: Lexington Books, 1972), p. 101.

14. Gordian Associates, Incorporated, "LDC Energy Supply/Demand Balances and Financing Requirements," Partial Draft Report, Prepared for Brookhaven National Laboratory (Upton, New York: BNL, 6 January 1978), pp. 3-20, 21.

15. Milton R. Benjamin, "South Korea Doubles Atomic Power Plans" *Washington Post,* 13 November 1978, p. 1.

16. Beier, *et. al, The Task Ahead,* pp. 52-54 and Dipak Mazumdar, *The Urban Informal Sector,* World Bank Staff Working Paper No. 211 (Washington, D.C.: World Bank, July 1975), Table 1, p. 4.

17. Mazumdar, *The Urban Informal Sector,* p. 10.

18. David Turnham and Ingelies Jaeger, *The Employment Problem in Less Developed*

Countries (Paris: Development Centre of the Organization for Economic Co-Operation and Development, 1971). pp. 96-97. Actually these authors use the term "household" to describe what we refer to as the informal sector.

19. Kenneth King, *The African Artisan* (New York: Teachers College Press, 1977), p. 198.

20. Lester R. Brown, *In the Human Interest* (New York: W.W. Norton and Company, 1974), p. 109.

21. Andrew M. Kamarck, "Sub-Saharan Africa in the 1980s: An Economic Profile," in *Africa: From Mystery to Maze*, ed. by Helen Kitchen (Lexington, Mass.: Lexington Books, 1976), Table V-6, p. 175

22. Jaycox, "La Pauvreté dans les Villes," p. 10-11, and *World Bank Annual Report, 1979*, p. 22.

23. *World Bank Operations Sectoral Programs and Policies* (Baltimore: Published for The International Bank for Reconstruction and Development by Johns Hopkins University Press, 1972), p. 421.

24. Erik P. Eckholm, *Losing Ground: Environmental Stress and World Food Prospects* (New York: W.W. Norton and Company, Inc. 1976), pp. 103-104.

25. Beier, *The Task Ahead*, p. 62.

26. Calculated from Population Reference Bureau's mid-1978 figures. These are based on U.S. population data. Note that definitions of urban and rural vary widely among countries, so that the rural proportion of the population may actually be somewhat underestimated.

27. Amulya Kumar N. Reddy, "Energy Options for the Third World," *Bulletin of the Atomic Scientists*, Vol. 34, No. 5, May 1978, p. 29.

28. Population Reference Bureau, Inc., 1978 "Population Data Sheet."

29. David Pimentel with the assistance of workshop participants, *Energy Needs, Uses and Resources in the Food System of Developing Countries,* (Ithaca, N.Y.: Cornell University, 23 December 1977), p. 11, and Roger Revelle, "Requirement for Energy in The Rural Areas of Developing Countries," in *Renewable Energy Resources and Rural Applications in the Developing World,* ed.

by Norman Brown (Boulder, Col.: Westview Press, 1978).

30. Eckholm, *Losing Ground,* pp. 102-3, 105-6.

31. *Ibid.*, p. 102.

32. *Ibid.*, p. 102 and Turi Hammer Dijernes, *Wood for Fuel, Energy Crisis Implying Desertification, The Case of Bara, The Sudan.* Published Dissertation, (Bergen Norway: Geografisk Institute, 1977); Arjun Makhijani, "Energy Policy for the Rural Third World" (London: International Institute for Environment and Development, September, 1976).

33. Reddy, "Energy Options," p. 29.

34. Makhijani, "Energy Policy," p. 10.

35. Reddy, "Energy Options," p. 29-30.

36. World Bank, *Rural Electrification,* October 1975.

37. Arjun Makhijani and Alan Poole, *Energy and Agriculture in the Rural Third World,* A Report to the Energy Policy Project of the Ford Foundation (Cambridge, Mass.: Ballinger Publishing Company, 1975).

38. World Bank, "Prospects for Traditional and Non-Conventional Energy Sources in Developing Countries," World Bank Staff Working Paper No. 346, prepared by David Hughart, Energy Dept. (Washington, D.C.: World Bank, 1979), p. 46.

39. For a fuller discussion of the issue in the South Asian context, see Iftikhar Ahmed, "The Green Revolution and Tractorization: Their Mutual Relations and Socio-Economic Effects" in *International Labour Review,* Vol. 114, No. 1, July-August 1976, pp. 83-93.

40. U.N.D.P., *Bangladesh Energy Study for the Government of Bangladesh,* Administered by the Asian Development Bank, November 1976; Digernes, *Wood for Fuel.*

41. Conversation with Robert E. Tsenin of Shell International, Inc., Planning Dept., Washington, D.C., 14 Sept. 1978.

42. World Bank, *Rural Electrification,* October 1975, p. 17.

43. World Bank, *Rural Electrification*, p. 18.

44. These figures include both "market" and "centrally planned" developing countries of which China is the most important. From *World Energy Supplies 1971-75*, Table 1.

45. A.K.N. Reddy and K.K. Prasad, "Technological Alternatives and the Indian Energy Crisis," in *The Economic and Political Weekly*, Special Number, August, 1977, pp. 1465-1502. Their 28,000 kCal/person/day estimate is based upon a paper done by Everett Hafner, "An Energy Budget," Hampshire College, 1971, mimeographed. Hafner's budget is a minimum energy needs assessment for an "average" American. His estimate was 31,000 kCal/day which Prasad and Reddy cut to 28,000 for the purposes of their exercise because India doesn't need the 3000 kCal amount included in the U.S. budget for space heating. Space heating needs for India can be picked up in cooking heat and/or extra clothing.

46. Developing country population estimates for the year 2000 are from Population Reference Bureau, Inc., "1978 Population Data Sheet" which is based on the U.N. medium variant projectors estimated in 1978. Population and energy figures include China.

47. Kirit Parikh, *Energy*, Second India Studies, (Delhi: The Macmillan Company of India Limited, 1976), p. 18. Percentages derived from energy consumption figures of the "Fuel Policy Committee Report" (of India) March (draft) and May, 1974 and "Energy Survey Committee Report," 1964.

48. World Bank, *Rural Electrification*.

49. World Energy Conference, Conservation Commission, *World Energy Resources, 1985-2020* (New York: IPC Science and Technology Press, 1978), pp. 64-71. Percentages are based on "geological resources" estimates submitted most recently to the World Energy Conference. "Geological resources" are defined by the authors as "within an order of magnitude that can be regarded as realistic for those resources that may some day be of economic interest [sic] for the population of the world." The authors suggest that this may be a better frame of reference than current technology and economics since these are both going through a period of rapid change and are in part a reflection of a lack of exploration and development particularly in the Third World.

50. Reddy, "Energy Options for the Third World."

51. Earl, *Forest Energy*, pp. 28-30.

52. *The Urban Edge* (published by the Council for International Liaison) Vol. 2, No. 2, Feb. 1978, pp. 3-5.

53. Report of the Secretary-General, "Recent Energy Trends and Future Prospects" (Geneva: UNECOSOC, Committee on Natural Resources, 9-20 May, 1977).

54. *Oil and Gas Journal*, 26 December 1977, pp. 100-101.

55. U.S. Department of Energy estimates from R. Taroslavsky and D. Farney, "Synthetic Fuel Plans Stir Doubts on Costs, Environmental Impact," in *Wall Street Journal*, July 12, 1979, p. 17.

56. Data compiled by Gordian Associates (Washington, D.C.) from Bernardo Grossling, *Window on Oil: A Survey of World Petroleum Resources* (London: The Financial Times, Ltd., 1976).

57. The World Bank's becoming more actively involved in other areas of petroleum. In 1977, it started a $500 million program of loans for petroleum development. But exploration is still not touched by banks. John Burgess, "Bankers Ready to Finance Large Viable Projects," *Asian Finance*, 15 July 1978, p. 33.

58. Amongst others see, U.S. National Academy of Sciences, *Energy and Climate: Outer Limits to Growth?* (Washington, D.C.: NAS Geophysics Research Board, 1977).

59. Report of the U.N. Secretary-General, "Recent Energy Trends."

60. For reserves and production see *International Petroleum Encyclopedia 1978* (Tulsa, Ok.: Petroleum Publishing Co., 1978). For uses of production, see Organization for Economic Co-Operation and Development, International Energy Agency, Standing Group on Long-Term Co-Operation, "Technical Report on the Energy Prospects for Developing Countries," No. IEA/SLT (78) 27 (Paris: 20 February, 1978), pp. 20-21.

61. See "Algerian LNG Puts Gas Pricing to a Test," *Business Weekly*, 6 March 1978, pp. 29-30.

62. OECD, "Technical Report on Energy

Prospects," p. 21.

63. Petroleum Industry Research Foundation, Inc., *Outlook for World Oil,* p.3.

64. U.N. Report of the Secretary-General, Committee on Natural Resources "Status and Prospects of Oil Shale Production and Utilization in Developed and Developing Countries" (New York: U.N. ECOSOC, E/C.7/73, 20 April 1977), p. 25.

65. J.A. Lane, "Nuclear Energy in the Developing Countries," in *Petroleum and Beyond,* ed. by Dick McDonald (London: Ontario University of Western Ontario, 1978), p. 86.

66. *Ibid.,* p. 84.

67. *Ibid.,* p. 86.

68. J.A. Lane, *et al.,* "Nuclear Power in Developing Countries," International Atomic Energy Agency (IAEA-CN-36/500).

69. For hydropower potential, see World Energy Conference, *Survey of Energy Resources,* 1974; for production see, U.N. *World Energy Supplies, 1971-1975.*

70. Adrian Lambertini, "Energy and Petroleum in Developing Countries, 1974-1980," World Bank Staff Working Paper No. 229 (Washington, D.C.: World Bank, February 1976), p. 14.

71. Efrain Friedman, Jr., "Energy Supply/Demand Outlook, 1980-5," Draft Report (Washington, D.C.: World Bank, 16 July 1974), p. 21.

72. Glenn E. Coury, *Status and Outlook of Geothermal Energy,* Report to World Bank, 7 March 1974.

73. United Nations, ESA/RTD *Energy,* pp. 11-12 in Arthur D. Little, Inc., *An Overview of Alternative Energy Sources for LDCs, Report to AID,* #C-77105, p. I-B-6.

74. H. Marvin, "Solar Cells" ERDA Announcement, 30 September 1977.

75. National Academy of Sciences (NAS), *Energy for Rural Development: Renewable Resources and Alternative Technologies for Developing Countries* (Washington, D.C.: NAS, 1976), p. 81.

76. *Depthnews Science Service* (Manila, Philippines, Press Foundation of Asia, 1 September 1977).

77. William Metz, "Solar Thermal Electricity: Power Tower Dominates Research," *Science,* 22 July 1977, pp. 353-356.

78. Alvin F. Hildebrandt and Lorin L. Vant-Hull, "Power with Heliostats," *Science,* 16 September 1977, pp. 1139-1146.

79. William von Arx, "Energy: Natural Limits and Abundances," *American Geophysical Union,* September, 1974.

80. Windcharger, Inc. (U.S.) markets the $450 model and American Energy Alternative, Inc. (U.S.), the 5KW model at $600/KW. Other marketers include Independent Power Developers, Inc. (U.S.) and Dunlite (Australia) amongst others.

81. Richard F. Curry, "Alcohol Fuels: An Alternative Energy Supply," *American Motorist Magazine,* September/October, 1977, pp. 4-5.

82. Figures for Nepal from Brookhaven National Laboratory, "A Preliminary Assessment of the Egyptian Energy Outlook," 1 February 1978. U.S. hydropower per capita installed capacity figure from U.N. *World Energy Supplies, 1971-1975.*

83. James E. Nickum, *Hydraulic Engineering and Water Resources in People's Republic of China,* U.S.-China Relations Report #2 1974.

84. Informal conversation with Mr. William Delp of Independent Power Developers, at Overseas Development Council, Fall 1977.

85. Bill Stout, *Energy for Global Agriculture* (Rome: FAO, forthcoming). Stout cites calculations suggesting that if an average draft animal (bullock or horse) generates 500 watts of power harnessed at 10% efficiency for 8 hours a day, 250 days a year, produces about 100 KWH annually, then the total estimated draft animal population of developing countries would produce more than 25 million MWH of energy.

86. Arjun Makhijani and Alan Poole, *Energy and Agriculture in the Third World* (Cambridge: Ballinger, 1975), p. 75; Informal U.S. Department of Agriculture estimates. Ashok V. Desai, "India's Energy Consumption, Composition and Trends" in *Energy Policy,* Sept. 1978, p. 222. His estimate was based on the Indian *National Sample Survey No. 65* (Delhi, 1962). One estimate gives draft animals working 151 days/year.

87. *IMF Survey,* 19 June 1978, pp. 179-182.

88. Martin McLaughlin and the Staff of Overseas Development Council, *The United*

States and World Development: Agenda 1979. Published for the Overseas Development Council (New York: Praeger Publishers, Inc., January, 1979), Annex E, Table E-24.

89. John C. Sawhill, Keichi Oshiwa and Hanns W. Maull, "Energy: Managing The Transition" (New York: Trilateral Commission, Triangle Paper:17), p. 57.

90. *Ibid.*, p. 68 footnote.

91. In this connection, a good discussion of the problems of trade adjustment assistance can be found in Charles R. Frank, Jr., "Adjustment Assistance: American Jobs and Trade with the Developing Countries" (Washington, D.C., Overseas Development Council, Development Paper 13, June 1978).

92. Speech by Harry Bridges, President, Shell Oil Corp., 19 October 1976.

93. Exxon Corp., "Exploration in Developing Countries" (Unpublished paper, June, 1978).

94. Roger D. Hansen and the Staff of the Overseas Development Council, *The U.S. and World Development: Agenda for Action 1976,* Published for the Overseas Development Council by Praeger Publishers, (New York: 1976), pp. 91-92, 115.

95. *Ibid.*, p. 116.

96. Sawhill, *et al.*, "Energy: Managing the Transition," pp. 89-90 and Hansen, *et al.*,

"Energy: *Agenda for Action: 1976,* p. 116.

97. Sawhill, *et al.*, "Energy: Managing the Transition," p. 77.

98. *Ibid.*, p. 60.

99. *Ibid.*, p. 84.

100. Solar energy is taken here to mean those sources of energy that are ultimately driven by the sun's radiation. They include: photosynthesis (biomass), wind, water and direct solar energy. Of course, all animate energy is dependent, indirectly and directly, upon solar energy as well.

101. Mr. Kissinger proposed the creation of an International Energy Institute in his statement to the Seventh Special Session of the U.N. General Assembly and later in his December 16, 1978 speech to the Conference on International Economic Cooperation (CIEC).

102. Sawhill, *et al.*, "Energy: Managing the Transition," p. 80.

103. Hansen, *et al.*, *Agenda for Action: 1976,* pp. 92-95.

104. Internally circulated proposal paper, James W. Howe, Overseas Development Council.

105. James W. Howe and the Staff of the Overseas Development Council, "Energy Problems of Developing Countries: Implications for U.S. Policy," final report to the Council on Environmental Quality, Contract No. EQ-7AC016 (unpublished), August, 1978.

CHAPTER FIVE

International Energy
Arrangements and the
Developing Countries

LINCOLN GORDON

In an extended analysis of international energy issues, the author has distinguished four sets of problems requiring policy attention at both national and international levels. They are summarized as follows:[1]

1) Completing adjustments to the economic consequences of the price discontinuity of 1973-74.
2) Protecting against the security dangers of supply interruptions and of nuclear proliferation.
3) Defining and moving toward some form of longer-term energy sources to replace cheap oil and gas.
4) Avoiding, minimizing or managing an oil supply and price crunch en route to the long-term alternative.

Events on the international energy scene—notably the shift from a buyers' to a sellers' market in late 1978 with the interruption of Iranian petroleum supplies and the formalization of price increases at the OPEC conference of June 26-28, 1979—have focused attention almost exclusively on the fourth set of issues. However, in all four cases current international arrangements do not provide adequately for the need or interests of the developing countries (LDCs), especially the more advanced ones now called "newly industrializing" (or NICs).

The principal sufferers from these institutional defects are the developing countries themselves, but a strong case can be made that arrangements more responsive to their interests would also be beneficial to the United States, the other industrial countries and the world economy and polity at large. This preliminary exploration of such questions is intended to provoke discussion.

Because of the current preoccupation with international oil prices and production levels, the issues will be discussed in reverse order from the outline summarized above. As a preliminary, however, it is helpful to recapitulate, in quantitative terms, the history and outlook of the developing countries' share in the world energy economy.

The LDCs and the World Energy Economy

The salient facts are summarized in Table 1 on pages 82-83, covering commercial energy consumption in all forms and liquid fuels separately. From the last two lines of each set of data, it will be seen that the share of LDCs (including the OPEC countries and China) in the world total has risen since 1955 from 9.5 to 17.9 percent for all commercial energy and from 12.4 to 17.1 percent for liquid fuels. (The OPEC countries account for only 2 percent of the total and 2.5 percent of the oil.)

It is also noteworthy that, while the sharp rise in prices at the end of 1973 reduced the consumption growth rates for both industrial and developing countries, the reduction was much greater for the industrial countries than for the LDCs. In fact, between 1973 and 1975, the industrial countries experienced a substantial absolute fall in consumption, while LDC consumption continued to grow at more than 5 percent a year.

This contrast reflects the partial delinking of overall economic growth rates between the developing and industrial countries. The delinking was made possible, in some cases, by very heavy international borrowing and, in others, by exceptionally good harvests or by the introduction of more effective domestic growth policies.

This contrast in energy consumption growth rates may also reflect a smaller price elasticity in the demand for commercial energy in the developing countries, resulting from the continuing replacement of traditional by commercial fuels and the more limited opportunities for energy conservation. It is intended to test this hypothesis both a) by comparing changes in ratios of energy consumption to overall output for a large number of countries and b) by examining the sectoral experience of some of the more advanced developing countries.

All energy projection scenarios for the rest of the century predict that annual consumption growth rates in LDCs will exceed those of the industrial countries by 2 to 4 percentage points. Since population growth in the LDCs continues at about 2.1 percent a year, compared with 0.7 percent for the industrial countries, simply maintaining equal growth in consumption per capita would account for half that differential.

The most serious analyses of long-term economic growth prospects in the industrial countries point to slower economic growth in the fourth quarter of this century than in the third. This is expected for a variety of reasons, including basic structural changes in demography and occupational patterns and plausible hypotheses concerning work-leisure tradeoffs, lesser gains in productivity, and consumption preferences. The prospect of higher energy costs is not a major factor in these projections, but it does tend to reinforce them. The kinds of structural changes under-way in the more dynamic LDCs, in contrast, portend continuing economic growth at relatively high rates and a correspondingly high growth in energy consumption.

This outlook might be reversed either by a major and long-lasting worldwide economic depression or by the unavailability of adequate energy supplies at costs no higher than those of long-term replacements for oil and gas—generally assumed to be in the range of $20 to $25 (in 1978 prices) per barrel of oil equivalent. In either of these cases, LDC energy consumption might grow only slowly or not at all. Assuming that an economic and social catastrophe (perhaps also leading to a political catastrophe)—whose avoidance should be a prime objective of national and international policies generally—can, in fact, be averted, a continued energy consumption growth differential of 3 points or more between in-dustrial and developing countries appears highly probable. If this is realized, the LDC share in world commercial energy consumption, just under 18 percent in 1976, would rise to about 25 percent by 1990 and to more than 30 percent by the end of the century. These are increases sufficiently large to have a major impact on market conditions. The pre-dominant role of LDCs on the supply side of the world oil market needs no emphasis. What does call for more thoughtful attention is their growing importance on the demand side.

The other striking feature of LDC commercial energy consumption is its high concentration in a small number of countries, especially the NICs and the two giants—China and India—where huge numbers offset rela-tively low intensities. Table 2 on page 84 lists the 20 LDCs (including oil exporters and centrally planned countries) with the highest aggregate consumption in 1976, while Table 3 on pages 86-87 focuses on the oil-importing market economy LDCs, listing the first ten in order of per capita consumption intensity. These ten, although representing less than one-fifth of the population of the group as a whole, account for half the group's total commercial energy consumption and almost three-fifths of its oil consumption. It is these two (overlapping) sets of countries that will be most affected by any international energy arrangements involving the LDCs. If some kind of international representation is required, it is likely to be furnished from these countries.

TABLE 1
World Energy and
Liquid Fuel Consumption
by Major Country Groupings,
1955-1976
(millions of metric tons of coal equivalent)

TOTAL COMMERCIAL ENERGY CONSUMPTION

	1955 Am't.	1955 % Share	1965 Am't	1965 % Share
1. WORLD TOTAL	3,243	100.0	5,212	100.0
2. Ind'l Market Countries	2,263	69.8	3,274	62.8
3. Developing Market Countries	203	6.3	389	7.5
4. Cent. Planned Countries	778	24.0	1,549	29.7
5. Asian Cent. Planned	105	3.2	339	6.5
6. Other Cent. Planned	673	20.8	1,210	23.2
7. All Industrial (2 + 6)	2,936	90.5	4,484	86.0
8. All Developing (3 + 5)	308	9.5	728	14.0

CONSUMPTION OF LIQUID FUELS

	1955 Am't.	1955 % Share	1965 Am't	1965 % Share
1. WORLD TOTAL	991	100.0	1,955	100.0
2. Ind'l Market Countries	764	77.1	1,429	73.1
3. Developing Market Countries	120	12.1	226	11.6
4. Cent. Planned Countries	107	10.8	300	15.3
5. Asian Cent. Planned	3	0.3	16	0.8
6. Other Cent. Planned	104	10.5	284	14.5
7. All Industrial (2 + 6)	868	87.6	1,713	87.6
8. All Developing (3 + 5)	123	12.4	242	12.4

SOURCE: United Nations, *World Energy Supplies, 1950-1974*
and *1972-1976*, Series J, Nos. 19 and 21, 1976 and 1978

1973		1975		1976		Growth Rates (%)			
Am't	% Share	Am't	% Share	Am't	% Share	1955 −76	1965 −76	1965 −73	1973 −76
7,767	100.0	7,877	100.0	8,318	100.0	4.6	4.3	5.1	2.3
4,829	62.2	4,640	58.9	4,902	58.9	3.7	3.7	5.0	0.5
711	9.2	785	10.0	846	10.2	7.0	7.3	7.8	6.0
2,227	28.7	2,452	31.1	2,570	30.9	5.9	4.7	4.6	4.9
554	7.1	618	7.8	647	7.8	9.0	6.1	6.3	5.3
1,673	21.5	1,834	23.3	1,923	23.1	5.1	4.3	4.1	4.8
6,502	83.7	6,474	82.2	6,825	82.1	4.1	3.9	4.8	1.6
1,265	16.3	1,403	17.8	1,493	17.9	7.8	6.7	7.2	5.7
3,572	100.0	3,496	100.0	3,733	100.0	6.5	6.1	7.8	1.5
2,528	70.8	2,329	66.6	2,491	66.7	5.8	5.2	7.4	−0.5
454	12.7	491	14.0	534	14.3	7.4	8.1	9.1	5.6
590	16.5	675	19.3	708	19.0	9.4	8.1	8.8	6.3
76	2.1	93	2.7	104	2.8	18.4	18.5	21.5	11.0
514	14.4	582	16.6	604	16.2	8.7	7.1	7.7	5.5
3,042	85.2	2,911	83.3	3,095	82.9	6.2	5.5	7.4	0.6
530	14.8	584	16.7	638	17.1	8.2	9.2	10.3	6.4

TABLE 2

The Twenty Largest LDC Energy Consumers, 1976

	Energy Consumption (thousands of metric tons of coal equivalent)	Population (mid-1976) (millions)	Per Capita Consumption (Kg. of coal equivalent)
1. China	590,062	835.8	706
2. India	132,924	620.4	214
3. Brazil	79,840	110.0	726
4. Mexico	76,501	62.0	1,234
5. North Korea	49,900	16.3	3,061
6. Iran	49,768	34.3	1,451
7. Argentina	46,404	25.7	1,806
8. South Korea	36,583	36.0	1,016
9. Venezuela	35,079	12.4	2,829
10. Indonesia	30,428	135.2	225
11. Turkey	29,830	41.2	724
12. Taiwan	27,547	16.3	1,690
13. Egypt	17,996	38.1	472
14. Saudi Arabia	17,561	8.6	2,042
15. Colombia	16,657	24.2	688
16. Philippines	14,380	43.3	332
17. Thailand	13,217	43.0	307
18. Pakistan	13,112	71.3	184
19. Algeria	12,608	16.2	778
20. Cuba	11,597	9.5	1,221
Total of Twenty Largest	1,299,709	2,199.8	591
Other Developing Countries	210,502	841.5	250
All Developing Countries	1,493,000	3,040.8	491
Share of Twenty in LDC Total (%)	87.1	72.4	——

Source: Energy Consumption data from United Nations, *World Energy Supplies, 1972-1976*, Statistical Papers Series J, No. 21, New York, 1978. Population data from International Bank for Reconstruction and Development, *World Development Report, 1978*, Table I. Data on Taiwan from U.S. Department of Commerce.

The LDCs and the Oil Market Squeeze

The world has experienced several years of growing complacency about short and medium-term oil market gluts, the erosion of OPEC prices by widening discounts and general inflation and ample margins of time in which to develop substitute supplies and conservation measures with full respect for environmental and other public concerns.

The events of 1979 again shocked the publics and governments of oil-importing countries into a "crisis" mentality. Reduced oil supplies from Iran and a more conservative attitude toward production ceilings in Saudi Arabia have created a sellers' market. These developments have permitted much larger general price increases by exporters than had been expected in late 1978 and fantastic price levels for some transactions in the spot market. Demand in the industrial countries may be reduced somewhat in direct response to higher prices and more by general economic recession (and possibly by deliberate conservation measures); but it now seems possible, although not certain, that OPEC members may trim supplies correspondingly to avoid downward price pressures.

At first in the agreement in the International Energy Agency (IEA) for 5 percent reductions in oil consumption, and then in the Tokyo Summit meeting of the Big Seven, the response of the industrial countries has been: 1) to establish country-by-country oil import ceilings, 2) to seek ways of reducing unbridled bidding up of the spot market and 3) to offer "to examine with oil-exporting countries how to define supply and demand prospects on the world oil market."[2] The Tokyo Summit communiqué also points to the bad effects of OPEC price increases on oil-importing LDCs and hints at the desirability of more OPEC financial aid.

For its part, the OPEC Conference communiqué of June 28, 1979, gives a good deal of lip service to concern for oil-importing developing countries, so much so as to suggest acute political sensitivity (at least on the part of some of the exporters) to complaints from the importers. Yet the $800 million proposed to be added to the OPEC special fund is less than one-tenth of the probable annual increase in OPEC revenues from LDCs resulting from recent price increases.

The OPEC Conference remanded for further study "another proposal for a long-term fund to be set up jointly by the industrialized countries and OPEC member countries to compensate developing countries for imported inflation, on the one hand, and any increases in crude oil prices on the other."[3] But the idea of a bilateral dialogue with industrial countries or a triangular dialogue with both industrial and developing importing countries is firmly rejected unless it deals not only with energy but also with general development problems, technology transfer, financial and monetary reforms, world trade and raw materials.

This amounts to a resuscitation of the position of 1975, when interna-

TABLE 3

Oil-Importing Developing Market Countries:
The Ten Most Intensive Energy Consumers (1976)
(consumption in thousands of metric tons of coal equivalent)

Countries or Territories	Aggregate Commercial Energy Consumption
All Developing Market Countries[a]	837,465
Oil Exporting Developing Market Countries or Territories (25)	298,654
Oil Importing Developing Market Countries or Territories (96)	538,811
The Ten Most Intensive:[b]	
1. Singapore	5,153
2. Argentina	46,404
3. Taiwan	27,547
4. Hong Kong	5,754
5. South Korea	36,583
6. Chile	10,323
7. Brazil	79,840
8. Turkey	29,830
9. Colombia	16,657
10. Peru	10,336
Total of the Ten	268,427
Total of 86 Others	270,384
Share of the Ten in the 96 (%)	49.8

[a] United Nations classification, subtracting Puerto Rico, U.S. Virgin Islands, Panama Canal Zone, Cuba, Netherlands Antilles, New Caledonia, Guam, and French Polynesia; and adding Taiwan.

[b] Limited to countries or territories with total consumption above 5 million tons coal equivalent. Rough approximation only.

[c] *Source:* Based on data from United Nations, *World Energy Supplies, 1972-1976,* Statistical Papers Series J, No. 21; New York, 1978; data for Taiwan from U.S. Department of Commerce.

Population (millions)	Per Capita Consumption (kilograms)	Liquid Fuel Consumption
1,987.9	421	518,317
431.8	692	189,072
1,557.9	346	329,245
2.3	2,262	5,148
25.7	1,804	32,626
16.3	1,690	20,000c
4.5	1,279	5,735
36.0	1,016	19,350
10.5	987	6,595
110.0	726	62,216
41.2	724	21,140
24.2	688	9,422
15.8	654	8,747
286.5	937	190,979
1,271.4	213	138,266
18.4	——	58.0

tional discussions of energy markets were made contingent on the parallel consideration in the Conference on International Economic Cooperation (CIEC) of other items on the "New International Economic Order" agenda of the "Group of 77" (the developing countries in the United Nations). It simply disregards the fact that almost two years of conversation in CIEC led virtually nowhere.

Whatever one's appraisal of the results, organized international arrangements do exist for the consideration of trade and money and technology transfer and non-energy raw materials. The large omission in this list is precisely the topic of energy, and it is energy prices and availabilities that now pose unique dangers to the continuing developmental prospects of many oil-importing LDCs. It is unlikely that they will be easily persuaded this time to maintain a solid political defense of OPEC pricing practices in the evanescent hope that, in some unspecified fashion, OPEC's bargaining power will be used to extract from the industrial world both large transfers of current income in payment for oil and also a variety of new economic concessions to LDCs in general.

If the importance of the energy sector had been as evident in 1945 as it is today, the UN family of international institutions would doubtless have included a specialized agency on energy, parallel with those on food, health, labor and education. Creation of such an agency has recently been advocated by an articulate Jamaican official with experience in both CIEC and the World Bank. [4]

Several factors militate against the viability of this kind of proposal under present conditions: Some of the proposed functions are already being performed by the International Atomic Energy Agency, the International Monetary Fund and the World Bank. There is widespread public criticism of the UN bureaucracy in the industrial countries. They would not take kindly to the idea of creating a new agency with its bills paid mainly by them, its staffing mainly from the LDCs, its annual general meeting a new forum for political debate of irrelevant issues and its output of uncertain value in improving the world conditions of energy supply, trade and use.

But if there is little prospect for either a triangular energy dialogue or a new global energy agency, how can the oil-importing LDCs make their needs known, their influence felt and their potential contribution to solutions acknowledged? In relation to OPEC, they have every reason to press for liberality in production decisions and moderation in pricing. In these respects, their interests coincide with industrial importers.

The LDCs might also have separate objectives such as a two-tier pricing system (at least for the poorer LDCs) or a much more generous "compensation" than the OPEC special fund. In relation to the OECD (or IEA) group, they stand to gain from any collective decisions for oil import restriction and conservation in the industrial world. But they may not be content with assurances that their needs will be "kept in mind" as the industrial countries bargain with each other on national import ceiling levels, emergency sharing and other measures.

The logic of their situation points to some sort of organization to represent their collective interests and pool their bargaining power—in effect an ODCOI (Organization of Developing Country Oil Importers). This development may be inhibited by fear of impairing the "unity" of the Group of 77 or by the kinds of ideological and other differences that have frustrated proposals for a "Third World Secretariat" for the Group of 77 itself.

Since the industrial countries would benefit from increased cohesion among the oil-importing LDCs, but are obviously not in a position to promote it directly, they might encourage it indirectly by inviting a representative group (drawn mainly or entirely from the lists in Tables 2 and 3) to consult regularly with the appropriate committees of the IEA. Members of that group might in turn develop organized contact with wider constituencies on a regional basis, perhaps under the auspices of the UN Regional Economic Commissions.

The initial topics of consultation would include data coordination (on which a beginning has already been made), together with any kinds of policies designed to affect markets: cooperation in conservation and import restriction; emergency sharing; dampening of the spot market and offsetting accidental or deliberate supply curtailments from specific exporters. At a minimum, that kind of development should reduce the concern of the oil-importing LDCs that their interests may be disregarded by the industrial countries. It could also become the seed for a future ODCOI. Or it could be the first step in developing the consumers' side of an eventual petroleum commodity agreement.

It is somewhat curious that oil importers have been so reluctant to organize themselves for fear of generating a "confrontational" posture toward OPEC, when the systematic organization of both exporters and importers is an essential component of the classic pattern of "ideal" commodity agreements that have been so strongly advocated by all the LDCs (including OPEC members).

There was a fleeting moment in 1974 when it seemed possible that a combination of price indexing to maintain the real purchasing power of a barrel of exported oil and the corresponding security for investment of petrodollar surpluses might have been negotiated with OPEC in return for assurances of supply continuity. At that time, too many Western economists and policymakers, including some high U.S. government officials, were convinced of the inherent weakness of OPEC and the certainty of a price collapse to permit a serious exploration of such a possibility.

By mid-1979, with public recriminations at their highest level and calls in vogue for securing political consensus within the United States by making OPEC a declared "enemy," such an exploration still seemed untimely. But if a combination of recession, conservation and vigorous alternative supply policies by the importers brings about another shift toward a buyers' market within the next few years, it would be well to have thought through both the substantive content and the institutional arrangements appropriate to a petroleum commodity arrangement.

The LDCs and the Energy Regime Transition

The definition of a longer-term energy regime to replace cheap oil and gas and the adoption of measures to accelerate its orderly achievement are much more the sum of a series of national policies than an inherently international set of issues. There is no reason to want or expect global uniformity in either the timing or the character of the transition.

Countries vary enormously in their needs, their indigenous resources of conventional and unconventional fossil fuels and water power, their suitability for exotic renewable technologies (such as biogas, biomass and alcohol, direct solar or wind), their attitudes toward and capabilities for handling nuclear energy, and their ability to find and pay for imported fuels or capital equipment. The first requirement in each case is to lay a foundation at the national level for a comprehensive energy policy through a systematic assessment of alternative patterns of both demand and supply, related to each country's broader development strategy.

International cooperation can help this series of transitions in several ways: education and training in needed skills; financial and technical assistance in resource exploration; information exchange and technological transfer for novel technologies, and investment in energy supply and distribution systems. In relation to LDCs, much of this activity can be readily fitted into the established framework of bilateral and multilateral aid programs, including those of the World Bank, the Regional Development Banks and the UN Development Programme.

An additional institution might be justified, by analogy with the International Fund for Agricultural Development (IFAD), if the OPEC members were prepared to finance it on a large scale. In this case, one might hope for OPEC funding of more than half the total, with the OECD countries contributing technical skills along with minority financing. Like the IFAD, the governing body of this "IFED" (International Fund for Energy Development) and the voting arrangements would be triangular in more or less equal proportions. In the absence of special OPEC financing, however, it is difficult to see a justification for creating a special IFED.

Whatever the financial arrangements, it is to be hoped that the administration of energy aid programs will be delegated to existing agencies. Energy development should be an integral part of wider development. The renewable energy technologies are closely connected with land use, water control, agriculture and forestry; and they should not be organized in separate compartments from those responsibilities. A country's expertise, competence in general developmental economics, and the administrative overhead machinery of the existing institutions are all relevant to energy assistance programs; their duplication in a new agency would be costly and wasteful of scarce skills.

A case can be made, on the other hand, for a low key international energy technical agency focused on data improvement, facilitation of training, and exchange of information on new technologies and their application. It might be sponsored jointly by the UNDP and the Development Banks, with voluntary participation by interested national governments and foundations working in this field. Such an arrangement could be analogous to the international agricultural centers and their Coordinating Group for International Agricultural Research (CGIAR). Since the energy field has no major problem of genetic experimentation or adaptation to a variety of local environments (except possibly for new type biomass crops, which should be handled by the agricultural network itself), a simpler type of institution should suffice. An International Energy Institute limited to these functions, and specifically debarred from involvement with oil market issues, might be generally acceptable.

The LDCs and Energy Security

The issues of energy security fall into two groups: protection against sudden supply interruptions and avoiding the diversion of nuclear energy facilities and materials to weapons purposes. For LDCs, as for industrial energy importers, the main recourse against supply interruption is diversification of sources, supplemented by modest stockpiling. International emergency sharing arrangements might offer an important additional reassurance. For this reason, it was suggested above that the proposed new machinery for dialogue between the IEA and oil-importing LDCs include that item on its agenda.

The subject of international institutional arrangements to minimize nuclear weapons proliferation could occupy many volumes, as demonstrated by the weight of documentation on this subject being assembled by the International Nuclear Fuel Cycle Evaluation (INFCE). The relevant points here are that the nuclear proliferation problem relates mainly to the same large energy users among LDCs already identified above and their voluntary and active participation are indispensable requisites to success in any durable non-proliferation regime. After conclusion of the INFCE in February, 1980, it may be assumed that the IAEA will continue as the principal international forum for consideration of these matters.

New forms of evolutionary institutional development are to be expected, both in rule-making and in some types of operation—in the earlier stages focused on fuel supply assurances, spent fuel storage, and waste management, and ultimately on reprocessing and enrichment. Export controls by suppliers of nuclear materials and technology can be an indispensable enforcing mechanism to back up such international arrangements including the LDCs. But they can no longer serve by themselves as adequate restraints on nuclear proliferation.

The Economic Consequences of Higher Oil Prices

In conclusion, we come back to the effects of higher oil prices on the development prospects of the oil-importing LDCs and the kinds of international arrangements that might help to minimize those effects. It was pointed out that the 1973-74 round of price increases was less damaging to most of the LDCs than had been feared. Some observers have expressed the hope that a similar experience will follow the 1979 round. Quantitative analyses are now being made in the IMF, the World Bank, various central banks, and the international commercial banks. The first impressions are pessimistic. They suggest that the resiliency of the Eurocurrency markets and the debt servicing capacity of important numbers of the LDCs may not suffice to avoid extremely damaging reductions in essential non-fuel imports, especially of capital equipment. In that case, much larger supplemental financing through official channels may be needed along with a more active program of debt rescheduling.

On the institutional side, no radical innovations appear called for, even though the scale of operations by existing institutions may have to be greatly enlarged. A two-tier price system, however, would be infinitely preferable to *ad hoc* financing arrangements, and no opportunity should be lost to persuade the OPEC members and other exporters of its desirability.

FOOTNOTES

1. Lincoln Gordon, Growth Policies and the International Order (New York: McGraw Hill for The 1980s Project/Council on Foreign Relations, 1979), p. 110.

2. See text of Seven Nation Economic Summit communiqué, *New York Times,* June 30, 1979.

3. See text of OPEC communiqué, *New York Times,* June 29, 1979.

4. Trevor A. Byer, "The End of the Paris Energy Dialogue and the Need for an International Energy Institute," *Energy Policy* (London), Vol. 6, No. 4, December 1978, pp. 254-276.

Appendixes

Workshop on Energy Futures of Developing Countries
Cairo, Egypt, January 26-30, 1979

THE AGENDA

The following brief statement summarizes those topics on which our Cairo workshop on "Energy Futures of Developing Countries" is designed to focus.

We are sending this "concept paper" and several longer background documents to you well in advance of the meeting in the hope that they will provide a common information base from which the workshop can move quickly to an in-depth discussion of the major policy issues.

The Demand for Energy in the Developing Countries

The analysis of energy demand is merely one window through which to examine differing development strategies in the developing nations. There are, in fact, many different paths to "development," which in turn imply differing degrees of energy interdependence. Choices involving more or less concentration on "self-reliance," "basic needs" and rapid modernization are reflected in different structures of demand for energy and differing emphases in the kinds of energy likely to be required.

The program for the first day's discussion will focus on:
- differences in development strategies
- differing patterns of economic growth
- projected rates of growth in the Third World
- trends in the ratio of energy use to growth rates
- trends in the differing demands for energy in modernizing urban, modernizing rural and isolated rural areas
- implications of deforestations (efforts to reduce deforestation on environmental grounds will increase demand for more "commercial" fuels and for renewable "biomass" systems)

The Supply of Energy for Developing Countries—
World Energy Situation Report

The energy demands of developing countries are still a marginal, but growing, factor in assessing the adequac of world energy supplies for the future. This marginality makes the non-energy-producing developing nations peculiarly vulnerable to fluctuations in price and availability in a "world market" that is controlled mostly by government decisions and industrial nation requirements. Development planning for each developing country, therefore, requires (a) an understanding of the world energy situation present and projected, and (b) a national judgment about possible choices among differing ways of meeting each nation's future energy demand.

Discussion in our second day sessions will thus logically fall into the following categories:

A. *World Energy Situation Report: Changing Prospects and Projections*
  - Oil and gas
  - Coal
  - Nuclear energy
  - Synthetic fuels
  - Renewable systems, including solar

B. *Issues in Development Planning*
  - Centralization versus decentralization in energy strategy
  - Exploration potentials, in developing countries and their offshore "economic zones"
  - How "energy interdependent" is it safe to be?
  - Issues of fairness: to developing nation importers, to developing nation exporters, to industrial nation importers
  - Patterns and problems of development in energy-rich developing countries
  - Nuclear proliferation and nuclear power

Policy Implications for International Cooperation

The final day's program will focus on the internal decisions (about development strategy and about fairness) and the international bargains (about access to other nations' markets, fuels, commodities, labor, capital and technology) required for rapid and equitable development. Relevant bargains affecting energy demand and supply in and for developing countries include:

  - International trade in energy, and its monetary fallout
  - The internationalization of price and supply decisions: What part will the non-energy-producing developing countries play?
  - Research and development on energy technologies that may be especially useful in developing countries
  - The role of foreign enterprises in energy resource exploration and development—in developing countries and offshore
  - Does the world need a global energy agency?

THE PARTICIPANTS

Workshop on Energy Futures of Developing Countries
January 26-30, 1979
Cairo, Egypt,

Ibrahim H. Abdel Rahman
Institute of National Planning
9 Talaat Harb St.
Cairo, Egypt

Tarik Alakeel
Riyadh, Saudi Arabia

Thornton F. Bradshaw, President
Atlantic Richfield Company
Box 2679, Terminal Annex
Los Angeles, California 90051

Albert Bressand
Centre d'Analyse et de Prevision
Ministere des Affaires Etrangeres
37 Quai d'Orsay
Paris 75007, France

Noel J. Brown, Director
New York Liaison Office
United Nations Environment Programme
866 United Nations Plaza
New York, N.Y. 10017

Harlan Cleveland, Director
Aspen Institute for Humanistic Studies
Program in International Affairs
P.O. Box 2820
Princeton, New Jersey 08540

Paul Doty, Director
Aspen Institute for Humanistic Studies
Program in Science, Technology
and Humanism
79 Boylston St.
Cambridge, Mass. 02138

Lawrence J. Ervin, Director
Programs and Evaluation
al Dir'iyyah Institute
1925 N. Lynn St
Arlington, Va. 22209

Jose Goldemberg
Universidade de Sao Paulo
Instituto Fisica, Ciudade
Universitaria, Caixa Postal 20516
Sao Paulo, Brazil

Ivan L. Head, President
International Development
Research Center
Box 8500
Ottawa K1G 3H9, Canada

James W. Howe, Senior Fellow
Overseas Development Council
1717 Massachusetts Ave., N.W.
Washington, D.C. 20036

William T. Marin, Executive Director
al Dir'iyyah Institute
1925 N. Lynn St
Arlington, Va. 22209

Zygmunt Nagorski, Vice President
Lehrman Institute;
Special Adviser, Aspen Institute for
Humanistic Studies
717 Fifth Ave.
New York, N.Y. 10022

Waldemar Nielsen
Special Adviser, Aspen Institute
for Humanistic Studies
717 Fifth Ave.
New York, N.Y. 10022

R.S. Odingo, Secretary
Kenya Academy of Sciences
University of Nairobi
Nairobi, Kenya

Keichi Oshima
7-3-1 Hongo
Dunkyo-ku
Tokyo 113, Japan

Kirit S. Parikh
  Indian Statistical Institute
  7 S.J.S. Sansanwal Marg
  New Delhi 110 029 India

Germanico Salgado
  Carlos Montufar 319
  Esquina Monitor Bellavista
  Quito, Ecuador

Ibrahim Shihata, Director
  The OPEC Special Fund
  Obere Donau Strasse 93
  Vienna 1020, Austria

Osorio Tafal
  Center for Economic and Social
    Studies of the Third World
  Corl. Porfirio Diaz 50
  Mexico 20 D.F., Mexico

Gary H. Toenniessen, Associate Director
  Agricultural Sciences, The Rockefeller
    Foundation
  1133 Avenue of the Americas
  New York, N.Y. 10036

Werner Ungerer
  Consul General of the Federal
    Republic of Germany
  460 Park Avenue
  New York, N.Y. 10022

John Vafai
  ALUMIRAN
  Pahlavi Rd. - Jame Jam Ave.
  IDRO
  Teheran, Iran

Eric Zausner
  Booz, Allen and Hamilton
  4330 F. W. Highway
  Bethesda, Md. 20014

Observers:
R. Thomas Hoffmann
  International Institute for
    Environment and Development
  Suite 501
  1302 Eighteenth St., N.W.
  Washington, D.C. 20036

J. Hollander
  Chairman of the Board
  Beijir Institute
  Sweden
  Mailing address:
    Lawrence Berkeley Labs,
    Berkeley, Ca. 94720

Dr. Abdullah
  Ministry of Petroleum
  Cairo, Egypt

Larence McFarrin
  U.S. Department of Energy
  Washington, D.C. 20545

Carlos Miranda
  Center for Economic and Social
    Studies of the Third World
  Corl. Porfirio Diaz 50
  Mexico 20 D.F., Mexico

Ruth Troeller
  Center for Economic and Social
    Studies of the Third World
  Corl. Porfirio Diaz 50
  Mexico 20 D.F., Mexico
  (Professor of Monetary Economics,
    University of Surrey)